NOTABLE CHEFS AND FOOD WRITERS ON
THEIR UNFORGETTABLE DINING EXPERIENCES

Creating a
Meal
You'll Love

Dear Erica,
May you always
create meals you love,
and be surrounded by
good friends.
Much luck with
your book project!

EDITED BY MARK CHIMSKY-LUSTIG

SELLERS
PUBLISHING

Creating a
Meal
You'll Love

To Joanna, Kimberly, and Haya, with love

Copyright © 2010 Sellers Publishing, Inc.
All rights reserved.

Sellers Publishing, Inc.
161 John Roberts Road, South Portland, Maine 04106
For ordering information:
(800) 625-3386 toll-free
(207) 772-6814 fax

Visit our Web site: www.sellerspublishing.com • E-mail: rsp@rsvp.com

Cover design by Rita Sowins
Cover photo by Stacey Cramp
Interior design by Faceout Studio

ISBN 13: 978-1-4162-0579-1
Library of Congress Control Number: 2010924614

No portion of this book may be reproduced, stored in a
retrieval system, or transmitted in any form or by any means,
mechanical, electronic, photocopying, recording, or otherwise,
without the written permission of the publisher.

10 9 8 7 6 5 4 3 2 1

Printed in the United States of America.

CONTENTS

INTRODUCTION

*If you could write about one unforgettable dining experience —
whether it's a meal you created or one that was created for you
— what would it be?*

At the heart of *Creating a Meal You'll Love* is this simple
question that was posed to a diverse range of celebrated chefs
and food writers. Their responses, revealed in the fascinating,
funny, intriguing, and unexpectedly personal essays that are
compiled in this book, point to the fact that the question
isn't so simple after all and that what we love about a
meal may not just have to do with ingredients, presentation,
or taste . . .

Which is not to say that there's not plenty here to make your
mouth water. The favorite dishes highlighted in *Creating a Meal
You'll Love* represent a tantalizing United Nations of cuisines,
from Jaden Hair's essay on the familial gamesmanship involved
in sharing Chinese fondue, known as "hot pot," to Ronald
Holden's valentine to lasagna bolognese as made by Enza at her
popular Cucina Siciliana restaurant in Seattle.

Some of the contributors have even included recipes with their
essays, and the culinary delights include Jansen Chan's Steamed
Chocolate Jasmine Cakes, Amy Sherman's Dutch baby, Leticia
Moreinos Schwartz's *Feijoada* (Meat and Black Bean Stew), Bart

Potenza's Ginger-Miso Stir-fry, Tracey Ryder's "Magic" Seasonal Risotto, and Jonathan King's Short Ribs, Bourguignon Style.

Other contributors' recipes are influenced by a wide variety of sources: Marcus Samuelsson serves up his "favorite spaghetti recipe," his mother's spaghetti with peas; Karen J. Coates presents her husband Jerry Redfern's Southeast Asian Curry Burgers as one of the dishes in a creative imagining of what she'd like her last supper to be; Mika Takeuchi offers up Pear and Cheese Crostini, inspired by her stay at a twelfth-century villa in the medieval village of Todi in Umbria, Italy; and Julee Rosso shares her interpretation in miniature of Julia Child's flourless chocolate cake recipe. You can create the meals they love, and hopefully these dishes will become favorites of yours as well.

During the process of editing and assembling these essays, I came to realize that food is as potent a touchstone as music, defining a moment in our lives so that it lives forever in memory. Just as a few musical notes can bring back a lost time, sometimes the meals we make can be portals into the past, too. A few months ago, I made my first Passover Seder, with a little help from my friends. My foray into making a pot of matzoh ball soup (gluten-free, no less!) evoked wonderful memories of my grandmother stirring her matzoh balls with a watchful eye, and placing the steaming bowl of soup in front of me as if it were a precious gift. And of course, it was. For my grandmother, food equaled love.

When I made my soup, I felt a thrill the first time the submerged globs of batter suddenly bobbed up to the surface of the chicken broth, no longer formless but compact and roundish, just the way I recalled my grandmother's had looked. In that moment I felt deeply connected to her, as if she was in the room with me, lovingly standing vigil over the pot with me.

In her essay for this book, Denise Vivaldo writes of the enduring connection between food and memory, "I've chronicled the most important moments of my life by the food or tastes I've enjoyed. The memories, sentiments, heartbreaks, and happy times are completely tied into what I was eating. Food memories keep my taste buds alive and hold my treasured moments so they're always vividly alive for me."

A few of the chefs and food writers who agreed to write about their most memorable meal sent me emails on the difficulty of the challenge. *How do you choose just one out of a lifetime of food memories?* they asked. Some were able to describe the one dish that rose to the top, above all the rest. Other respondents didn't even try and, instead, ended up describing multiple meals. Often, the choices weren't about the most succulent this or the most unusual that, but about the emotions the meals conjured up.

As the essays from contributors began wending their way into my email "in" box, what I was pleased to discover was how personal and sometimes deeply moving they were. As the chefs and food writers focused on their most unforgettable dining experiences, they dug deep into their memories and revealed the ones that had had a profound effect on them. In many cases, I found that their essays were as much about the human connections they experienced as they were about the meal. That's ultimately what unites these essays — the way a favorite meal transports each contributor to another time and place, and to interactions that infuse the meal with meaning.

Some essays chart the course of a life — Anna Thomas takes the reader on an entertaining journey of her personal passages, represented by the meals she created in the different homes she lived in. Wendy Lyn, who grew up in the Deep South, shows how the life lessons her grandfather taught her when she was a child resonate for her as an adult as she tries to get her bearings after relocating to Paris. Michael Laiskonis maps out significant meals in ten different "courses" in a variety of far-flung places. He takes us from a market stall in Bangkok to lunches at Pierre Gagnaire and L'Arpège in Paris, all the while providing beautifully observed moments of being. He reveals the satisfaction of a quiet, solitary meal on Christmas Eve after an exhausting day of baking; the bliss of tasting the bounty collected from Paris's top pastry houses "all in the name of research"; and the pleasure of reflecting on the world with his wife while stopping for blueberry pie at a roadside shack overlooking the Massachusetts coastline.

As it turns out, without any direction from me, the essays cover the full spectrum of life experiences, encompassing childhood (Skye Gyngell's moving memory of being a seventeen-year-old sharing a dessert of "perfect" peaches with her father at a trattoria outside of Florence); early adulthood (David Sax's humorous account of coming under the thrall of Emeril Lagasse and the Food Network when he was a college freshman laid up with mono); new love (Shauna James Ahern's funny and heartfelt account of the first meal she made with the man who would become her husband); adopting a first pet (Louisa Chu's rollicking account of her dog's near-death experience in the south of France and how a crêperie owner delivered her own version of room service to their hotel); and new parenthood (Susur Lee's charming portrait of the culinary epiphanies he experienced when he and his wife trekked to Thailand with their six-month-old son).

Two pieces deal with a meal and its associations with the death of a parent — Raghavan Iyer presents an intensely powerful look at the traditional Indian ceremony surrounding the death of his father; we see how food is integral to the grieving process that prepares the deceased for the afterlife and the living for life after mourning. Jeanne Horak-Douriff creates a memorable depiction of taking over the Christmas feast that her late mother had made with such love in years past. It is a haunting essay that reveals how a meal can offer sustenance that is both spiritual as well as physical.

Though these rites of passage emerge in the essays, the book isn't structured around them. I thought that such a guiding principle might be too predictable, and I wanted this collection to be filled with the same element of discovery that I felt when I read each essay for the first time. I didn't want the essays hemmed in by an expected chronology. And so these pieces are assembled in a way that hopefully will be surprising and satisfying, with an essay on the loss of a loved one (Raghavan Iyer's "Brahmin Soul Food") next to an essay about the joys of cooking a meal for one's family (Michael Paley's "White-Apron Syndrome").

Even in an eclectic range of essays, commonalities abound. One surprise was the recurring popularity of eggplant — a number of the essays in the book make prominent or passing mention of this sturdy, versatile staple. It pops up in everything from a classic eggplant parmesan, courtesy of Denise Vivaldo, to *Timballo di Melanzane e Bucatini* (Eggplant and Bucatini Casserole), a dish that was served to Mary Ann Esposito at a dinner hosted by a baron and baronessa at their palazzo in Palermo, Italy. She also includes a recreation of this recipe — candelabras are optional.

Some of the essays share other aspects in common as well. Thailand is a destination of choice for several writers, as is Tokyo's famous Tsukiji Fish Market, one of the largest such markets in the world.

Many of the essays deal with the rich variety of friendships that add spice to a meal and one's life — Nick Malgieri on sharing a dinner with legendary chef Richard Olney in his cramped farmhouse just north of Toulon; Mimi Sheraton on the comforts of constancy and enduring friendship when hosting annual holiday celebrations; Jonathan King on turning a lazy Sunday afternoon into the occasion for a wonderfully spontaneous feast for friends.

Putting this collection together taught me about how our memories of food anchor us in the past, helping us to vividly recall the smile of a loved one or the way the guests at our table raised their glasses in a toast. Yet there is something about that fondly remembered dish that takes on a timeless quality as well. More than one contributor to this book suddenly switched from the past tense to the present tense when describing a meal they loved. I began to understand the power of such food memories — they are forever fresh, immediate in the mind's eye, as if we are experiencing that familiar dish for the very first time. As Michael Laiskonis wrote in an email to me about his change in verb tenses: "A dish is of the moment (past) but the memory of it seems to hang in the air in the present."

In *Creating a Meal You'll Love* the contributors bring their food memories vividly to life, enticing us with delectable dishes and insights about what truly made them special. My hope is that as you read their essays, you will take up the challenge of answering the question at the beginning of this introduction — each in your own way — and that the unforgettable meals you recall will bring back cherished memories that will delight and nourish you for a lifetime.

Mark Chimsky-Lustig
July 2010

South African-born **Jeanne Horak-Druiff's** internationally praised blog CookSister! was named as one of the Times Online's "Top 50 Food Blogs in the World" and is also a four-time winner of the Best South African Food Blog category in the South African Blog Awards. Her writing has been published in *Digital Dish,* National Geographic's *Food Journeys of a Lifetime,* and the *BloggerAid Cook Book.* She is a regular columnist in the online publication We Magazine for Women and South Africa's hugely popular Web site Food24 and has spoken at food-blogging conferences in the U.K. and South Africa.

THE TASTES OF
CHRISTMAS PAST

Jeanne Horak-Druiff

What do you do when you miss somebody who you'll never see again? When your head is full of questions that you still want to ask them, questions that had not even been formulated when you said goodbye? When your arms ache to be around them? When your ears strain to catch the memory of their voice, your nose, the memory of their scent? I'm afraid I'm not the burning bush and I don't have the answers. All I can tell you is what I do: I cook.

I am an obsessive recorder of events, both in writing and on film. One look at my numerous boxes and albums of photos will confirm this beyond a shadow of a doubt. My husband sees it as some sort of dysfunctional hoarding instinct — I see it very much like pressing flowers between the pages of a book. It is my way of trying to capture a fleeting moment or emotion, to record an event that will later seem as dim and distant as something viewed through the wrong end of a dusty telescope. One glance at a photograph of the day and everything comes back in sharp focus.

Next to my telephone is a photograph of me with my family on Christmas Day 2002: my brother, my dad, my darling sister-in-law, my nephew (who was less than a month old at the time), and Mamma sitting directly in front of me. I see it every day, but at Christmas time I seem to look at it more frequently because this was the last Christmas that Mamma was alive, and I miss her more at this time of year than any other. I don't think any of us realized that she was the glue that held our Christmas celebrations together and that, without her, nothing would ever be the same again. I think often about how our family Christmas routine was as fixed as the stars in the firmament (but no less eagerly anticipated for all that!) and how I never thought it could ever change. How wrong I was.

We always celebrated a family Christmas at home in South Africa. I can count on the fingers of one hand the Christmases we spent away from home while Mamma was alive. One time, I was alone with my husband in London, shivering with cold and yearning for our families. And one year my father had the deranged idea of spending a family Christmas at sea, aboard the ill-fated Achille Lauro cruise ship. (This was two years after the vessel's infamous hijacking and seven years before it sank off the coast of Somalia, so you can see why I describe the idea as deranged!) Suffice to say that at the time of booking, he was unaware that he was the only salty sea dog among us. He had to enjoy the Christmas dinner alone at his table while the rest of us prayed for a swift death in our bunks, overcome by seasickness! For years after that, I referred to him as "the Grinch who stole Christmas." To me, Christmas meant home, and celebrating anywhere else was simply not Christmas.

On the 24th, Mamma would retrieve from the fridge the gammon (a joint of pork meat, similar to a ham, which is always brine-cured and sometimes smoked) that she had selected for that year's feast and put it in the oven for what seemed to me like an eternity. By evening, the entire house would be redolent with the mouth-watering smell of slowly cooking smoked pork and that, to me, would always signal the true start of Christmas celebrations. On Christmas morning my brother and I were always up at the crack of dawn and racing to the Christmas tree before we were even properly awake. But the only things we were allowed to open then were our lucky packets — rather like two giant Christmas "crackers" — shoebox-like boxes in fancy Christmas colors, full of cheapish toys that would amuse small kids long enough to keep them off the wrapped presents, at least until our parents woke up. At 8:00 a.m. we were allowed to take our (oversized!) stockings of gifts from Father Christmas through to our parents' room and wake them up so that they could watch us slowly extract and examine each gift. Once we were all dressed and ready, my parents would annoyingly insist that we all had to sit at the table and have tea and mince pies before finally heading for the tree and its treasure trove of gifts. And only after all the presents had been opened and thoroughly inspected, could we move on to the next stage: the feast!

We had the same Christmas lunch pretty much my whole life, with only the starters and desserts varying slightly. After the gift-opening, Mamma would head for the kitchen and remove from the fridge the enormous cooked gammon, ready to be glazed. She would glaze it and I would help her decorate it with whole cloves, pineapple rings, and glacé cherries.

Together with the gammon would be a selection of salads, which also remained pretty constant through the years. There would be a salad of tinned white asparagus that would coolly slip down your throat in the summer heat. There was always a warm potato salad, rather than the more traditional cold one. This came about one year when Mamma forgot about making the potato salad until the food was practically on the table and, in her haste, used the still-hot potatoes to cobble together a warm potato salad. My brother liked it so much that it became a family tradition, to the extent that some years the cold potato salad had to be microwaved to achieve the right level of heat. On the sweet side, there were always watermelon balls that would crunch coolly between your teeth, and a cantaloupe and seedless white grape salad, which delighted us with its contrast between the yielding flesh of the melon and the delicious pop of the grape skins between our teeth. Once my brother's wife-to-be started joining our Christmas celebrations, she added another component that was to become a fixture: her seven-layer salad, consisting of crisp layers of diced vegetables topped with decadent mayonnaise, cheese, and crispy garlic croutons.

The starter varied: from my Mamma's famous and often-requested boozy chicken liver paté, to smoked salmon mousse wrapped in smoked salmon that my Mamma and I had painstakingly reverse-engineered after having it at a restaurant, to a simple plate of cold *antipasti*. And then came the main event. First my dad would open the Champagne, shooting the cork right into the garden, where my brother would always be waiting to catch it; then he would get down to the serious business of carving the cold gammon. I remember the Christmas gammon being one of the tastiest things in the world. I loved the saltiness of the meat, the sweet stickiness of the glaze, and the yielding, delicious layer of fat. It tasted like home and family and laughter and love to me. Afterwards, there was always dessert — usually Christmas pudding with my Mamma's homemade brandy sauce, or a strawberry pavlova. But to me, the gammon was the thing; that was the taste of Christmas and I doubt whether that will ever change.

When Mamma passed away, she had already selected the gammon for a Christmas meal that she would not live to see. I found it in the freezer that Christmas when I went home and it was the first gammon I cooked, as a tribute to my Mamma and as a source of comfort, both for myself and for my family. I realized then how many things I had never gotten around to asking my Mamma — things like, *Why did you never study medicine? Did you ever regret breaking off your engagement? How do you go about roasting a Christmas gammon? What the heck goes into the glaze? How do you get the fat cooked just right?* So many questions, but no Mamma to ask. I think that's the first time I realized how irretrievably gone she was, and how Christmas as I had always known it would never happen again.

The instructions were not written down in her dog-eared recipe index book, so I was left to rely on my own instincts and advice from friends as to how to go about creating a meal that would, in some small measure, make that first Christmas a little more bearable for us. The recipe lived in Mamma's head but, like her ample hips and slim wrists, she seems to have passed it on to me like a genetic imprint. In the intervening years, I have come pretty close to perfecting Mamma's roast gammon and every year when I cook it, I feel as if my Mamma is there with me, even if only for a little while. It's the one ritual from our lost family Christmases that I can carry with me wherever I go, and I let the taste and the smell of the gammon carry me away to another time.

A seasoned food professional with over twenty-five years of experience, **Denise Vivaldo** has catered more than 10,000 parties and has cooked for such guests as George H.W. Bush, Ronald Reagan, Prince Charles, Bette Midler, Cher, Sylvester Stallone, Arnold Schwarzenegger, and Maria Shriver. She began her culinary training at the Ritz Escoffier and La Varenne in Paris, and then graduated Chef de Cuisine from the California Culinary Academy in San Francisco. Denise spent numerous years as a professor at UCLA's Culinary Program and at her alma mater, the California Culinary Academy. She is the author of a number of popular books, including the IACP Award-winning *Do It For Less! Weddings*. Denise has also helped celebrities like Suzanne Somers, Richard Simmons, Susan Powter, and Jorge Cruise with their cookbooks.

FOOD MEMORIES

Denise Vivaldo

As a chef and caterer for over twenty-five years, I've cooked a lot of meals. Cooking has been my passion as well as my career for my entire adult life. I couldn't have done anything else. My personality fits this work, and I'm entirely grateful that I get paid to do it.

Cooking has kept me out of trouble.

At the wise old age of fifty-eight, nothing makes me sadder than to see and to listen to people tell me they don't have time to cook. That's like telling me they don't have time to breathe, love, or enjoy their life. Food, cooking, and feeding myself, family, and friends are the reasons why I get up every day. I've chronicled the most important moments of my life by the food or tastes I've enjoyed. The memories, sentiments, heartbreaks, and happy times are completely tied into what I was eating. Food memories keep my taste buds alive and hold my treasured moments so they're always vividly alive for me.

Here's a clear example: getting engaged to my first husband at twenty years old.

We were in a little Italian restaurant in Mill Valley, California. It was 1969. I was pretty and he was trying to avoid the draft. I barely remember what he said, and I did think the diamond was small, but the eggplant parmesan that night was perfect. We were married for seven years. It was a lifetime ago, and that young woman is long gone, and the tiny diamond has been reset, but I still cook the eggplant parmesan today and it is inspired by that moment. It was a happy moment, regardless of the outcome. Soft, warm, breaded eggplant, several melted cheeses, and garlicky tomato sauce with layers of herbs and mushrooms. Who could forget that?

I've studied food since I was that new bride. As a wedding present I was given *Mastering the Art of French Cooking* by Julia Child, Simone Beck, and Louisette Berthole. I started cooking a recipe every weekend. We were poor (he was a dental student), but we had to eat. It wasn't easy on my food budget, but cooking Julia's recipes became a necessity for me. I did not know French food since I'd grown up in an Italian family, but Julia showed me the way. I remember my first *Blanquette de Veau*, a creamy veal stew; I served it with a white

Burgundy (finding a white Burgundy in 1971 in San Rafael, California, wasn't easy, but I was determined). When friends came for dinner, they were amazed and so was I. That dinner took us to another place. We would never be the same again. Julia's recipe made us smart, grown up, and eager to search for more new sensations and adventures in food. Years later, when I worked with Julia and told her about that dinner, she simply replied, "Well done!"

I enrolled in the California Culinary Academy in San Francisco when my marriage was over, and found that my cooking was alive and well. I didn't want to cook in a restaurant but dreamed of giving parties: big, fancy, beautiful parties with white linens, tapered candles, delicious foods, and the world's finest wines. I practiced on my classmates and we planned meals together each weekend. We taught each other — through our mistakes and triumphs — how important perfected recipes were, the timing of every dish, how much to serve, and what foods taste the best together. It was a stunning time in my life. I realized that all food was not equal and that the preparation of a simple dish could be a meaningful experience. I also learned that in my life's tapestry, food was the thread.

My life has been richer, deeper, and sweeter from cooking.

In my career, fitness expert and bestselling cookbook author Richard Simmons has been a friend and client of mine for many years. When his mother, Shirley, passed away, he found a box of her recipe cards. He showed them to me and I saw that Shirley had attached a note saying, "For you, Dickie." When Richard was writing one of his many cookbooks, he asked me to test some of her recipes. I cooked for several days and then brought the finished recipes and dishes up to his home. With every bite of a dish, Richard would tell me something from his childhood, or a story about his mother and her great talent as a showgirl. We were laughing, crying, and eating all at the same time. My proudest moment ever was Richard telling me that my cabbage rolls were almost as good as Shirley's. And that's what we named the recipe, "Almost As Good As Shirley's."

I didn't have the opportunity to meet Shirley, but I only had to cook her food to know how much she loved her life and her son. She was still there. I know you're probably thinking, that's a lot to learn from cabbage, but trust me, that's the magic of a good dish.

Teaching cooking classes all around the world has taught me that cooking is a gift I've given myself. No matter what city, country, or continent I'm in, I get to create memorable meals that I love. Sometimes I cook them, sometimes I find them, and often I'm invited to them. It doesn't really matter. It's the sharing of food and eating that makes me happy.

What follows is my favorite recipe for very simple eggplant Parmesan. If you are reading this and don't cook, start here! Go right now to the store and buy the ingredients, a bottle of red wine, and toss a green salad. Go on now; create your own meal to love.

EGGPLANT PARMESAN   *Serves 4*

1 large egg
½ cup panko (Japanese-style) breadcrumbs (regular are fine, too)
½ cup finely grated Parmesan cheese
1 teaspoon chopped fresh oregano (or ½ teaspoon dried)
1 tablespoon torn fresh basil
Kosher salt and freshly ground black pepper
1 large eggplant, peeled and sliced into ½-inch rounds
3 cups chunky tomato sauce of your choice
1 pound crimini or button mushrooms, quartered and sautéed in 2 to 3 tablespoons olive oil
1 cup shredded or sliced mozzarella cheese

Preheat oven to 375°F. Line two baking sheets with parchment paper.

In a bowl, whisk the egg with 2 tablespoons of water.

In another bowl, combine the breadcrumbs, Parmesan, oregano, and basil. Season to taste with salt and pepper.

Dip the sliced eggplant first into the egg mixture, then into the breadcrumb mixture, and place on prepared baking sheets. Bake, turning once, until golden brown on both sides, about 25 minutes. Remove from the oven.

Increase oven temperature to 400°F. Spray a 9 x 13-inch baking dish with nonstick cooking spray. Spread a small amount of tomato sauce on the bottom. Place a layer of eggplant on top of the sauce, cover with a layer of mushrooms, and top with the mozzarella and sauce. Repeat this process with 2 to 3 layers until all the eggplant is in the dish. Top with the remaining sauce and mozzarella (and any leftover breadcrumb mixture).

Bake, uncovered, until the cheese is bubbly and golden brown, about 20 minutes. Enjoy!

ℰↃ   ℰↃ   ℰↃ

My tips:

Find eggplants with smooth, purple skins. They don't have to be big. When slicing one, take a bite and make sure it isn't bitter. If it is slightly bitter, salt the eggplant, let the slices sit on a plate, pour off the water, and blot dry before breading.

To save some time, buy a jar of chunky tomato sauce. Buy a plain flavor and then add sautéed garlic and some fresh rosemary, then cook it down with a half-cup of red wine. It tastes almost as good as homemade.

If the budget allows, use fresh buffalo mozzarella along with the grated Parmesan. It costs more but it's so worth it.

Nick Malgieri, former executive pastry chef at Windows on the World and 1996 inductee into Who's Who of Food and Beverage in America, is currently director of the baking program at the Institute of Culinary Education in New York City. The author of *BAKE!* and nine other cookbooks, including the James Beard Foundation Award-winning *How to Bake* and the IACP/ Julia Child Cookbook Award-winning *Chocolate,* Nick's recipes have been published widely, including in the *New York Times,* the *Chicago Tribune,* the *Washington Post, Food & Wine, Gourmet,* and *Bon Appétit.* He is a contributing editor of *Dessert Professional,* a frequent contributor to *Saveur,* and writes a monthly column for Tribune Media Services. Nick has appeared on national morning shows and local television throughout the United States, as well as on Food Network and Martha Stewart. Visit Nick's website at www.nickmalgieri.com.

DINNER AT RICHARD'S

Nick Malgieri

"You like all that awful sweet stuff?" Richard Olney had asked me in an accusing tone — he was a sworn hater of desserts. Now, after my first summer season working as a *commis pâtissier* (assistant pastry cook) at the Sporting Club in Monte Carlo, I was making my second pilgrimage to visit him; it was September 1974, right before I was to return and seek work in New York. The train ride from Monaco via Nice to Toulon was more than two-and-a-half hours long and I fell to thinking about our first meeting when I had accepted an invitation to visit after writing him a fan letter. It had been the previous spring and my recollection of the dinner was a blur of asparagus with lemon and local olive oil; a quickly roasted lamb loin with some tiny green beans; and cheese, of course, for dessert along with the fourth or fifth wine of the evening. Dinner was followed by many unfiltered Gauloises and much paternal advice about my desire to become a teacher and writer on baking. "Well, just watch out in that world of New York food people — it's a nest of vipers," Richard had warned.

As I boarded a bus a few blocks from the Toulon train station to continue my journey, I was already wondering what dinner would be like. The ride to the tiny village of Solliès-Toucas was fairly short and once there I found myself struggling to read my scribbled directions to his hillside farmhouse while bearing an immense bouquet of laurel leaves, partly because I knew he would use them in his famously gigantic *bouquets garnis*, and partly because, of anyone I had met or even read, I realized he deserved a crown of them. Climbing the steep path was an effort, though Richard, who never learned to drive, ran up and down the hill several times a day for shopping and errands. Finally at my destination, I was about to enter the basically one-room farmhouse when I saw that Richard was talking animatedly on a telephone — an addition since my last visit. I took a seat on one of the chairs at the table under the grape arbor and waited while he finished his call.

"That was Naomi Barry," Richard announced as he joined me outside, naming *Gourmet* magazine's then-Paris restaurant critic. He looked as he had on my first visit — French workman's shorts and an unbuttoned cotton shirt knotted at the waist. Instead of shoes, Richard favored thoroughly worn espadrilles in some garish color like turquoise, which made him walk slanted forward (to keep them on his feet), looking as though he were about to topple over.

After a short talk, we headed for the village, shopped for dinner, and made a quick visit with his friends, the Garins, who had moved south from Paris to open a casual restaurant nearby. Georges Garin had been the chef/owner of a celebrated Paris restaurant and he was the first chef for whom Richard had cooked a meal. Garin had pronounced the meal brilliant in every respect, of course.

Back up the hill, it was time for Champagne. I don't think Richard ever kept a bottle of Champagne at his bedside as the legendary chef Fernand Point had done, but I'm sure the thought must have crossed his mind. Indoors again, we sipped Champagne while Richard prepared one of his favorite first courses for late summer and early fall — a salad of figs and prosciutto with mint and a lemon crème fraîche dressing. Richard cut prosciutto into thin shreds, and I rinsed some wild mushrooms that would accompany a plump duck he had bought on our expedition. The mushrooms were ready and the duck was safely in the oven as I thought about my good fortune to know Richard, the only American ever recognized by the upper echelons of the French food world to the extent that he wrote a monthly column for the then-prestigious magazine *Cuisine et Vins de France*.

"Shall we start with an Yquem with the figs?" he asked as we crossed the patio to the wine cellar, hewn out of the side of an immense boulder opposite the house. He was talking about France's (and the world's) most precious and costly sweet wine. "The Marquis [de Lur-Saluces, owner of Chateau d'Yquem] has just sent me a case of these lovely half bottles." I boldly asked for a repeat of the almost as precious Château Talbot, guessing that it would work as well with the duck as it had months before with our roast lamb. He agreed and, on the way back to the house, he opened the screen door of his cheese locker, about the size of a large medicine cabinet, and selected three or four cheeses for dessert.

Back in the kitchen Richard deftly and repeatedly turned and basted the duck, then we started with the salad. Being Italian American, I had certainly eaten figs with prosciutto dozens of times at home, but never with mint or any kind of dressing. The interplay of the slight acidity of the lemon and cream, the figs' sweetness, and the prosciutto's deep saltiness was accented by slight but aggressive jolts of mint. The wine seemed like a thick scented honey and married perfectly with the boldly, yet subtly, seasoned salad.

The duck emerged crisp and deeply tanned from the oven and was put aside to rest before being carved. Meanwhile, Richard sautéed the mushrooms in butter with a *persillade*, a finely chopped mixture of garlic and parsley, one hand on the pan of mushrooms and the other on the now-empty roasting pan, deglazing the bits of browned duck flavor with the juice of some small sour oranges to make a simple sauce. A squeeze of lemon over the mushrooms and the main course was ready. Pretty full (and very tipsy) after half a bottle of Champagne and the rich salad and Yquem, I tore into the rare duck and the garlicky mushrooms. After almost six months in Monaco and France I had learned to eat almost everything blood rare.

"Keep the mushrooms away from the duck's sauce — when they flow together on the plate the result is far too acidic," Richard cautioned. The Talbot suffered a little from all that acidity and it was then I realized that, even though I believed he was a genius, Richard could cook in an entirely fallible manner.

"I think we need a change of pace with the cheese," he said, departing for the wine cellar, flashlight in hand. Here my memory starts to blur; I know there was more red wine and certainly all of Richard's favorite cheeses, especially that large, truncated pyramid of goat cheese covered with a kind of mold that looks like long white worms curled across its surface. I guess I politely ate some cheese and pretended to drink a little more wine, but my head was reeling — not only from the wine and food, but from the realization that I had just enjoyed the experience of a lifetime.

I must have crawled to the little book-lined alcove that held the guest bed, noticing in my stupor that Richard owned a copy in French of the autobiography of Heinrich Schliemann, who had excavated Troy. Richard's bed was right in the kitchen and the foot of the bed almost touched the dining table.

I awoke the next morning to the sound of Richard doing dishes in the miniscule sink cut from a single piece of local stone. Over coffee we discussed his impending book tour for *Simple French Food,* his second book. I even got to see portions of a carbon copy of the manuscript that Richard had saved and I read a little, realizing that Richard's voice in the book was as easily articulate and accurate as when he spoke. Before I left for the return to Monaco he suggested I stop by in early December to one of his classes at James Beard's house in New York, where he planned to promote the book. But that's another meal . . . and another story.

A celebrated chef, restaurateur, and philanthropist, **Susur Lee's** first job in the hospitality industry was as a fifteen-year-old apprentice at Hong Kong's Peninsula Hotel. After immigrating to Canada in 1978, Susur went on to become the executive chef of a number of restaurants and soon began attracting attention for his talents in the kitchen. One of *Food & Wine* magazine's "Ten Chefs of the Millennium," Susur has received many accolades for his popular restaurants — including Toronto's Madeline's and Lee, New York's Shang, and Washington, D.C.'s Zentan — all of which showcase his unique approach to Asian cuisine.

INSPIRED BY AN IDEAL MEAL:
A LOVE STORY OF FAMILY, FOOD,
AND GOOD FORTUNE

Susur Lee

About twenty years ago, when my eldest son, Levi, was six months old, my wife and I decided, "What the hell, let's go to Thailand!"

It wasn't until we had booked the airline tickets that I started to have nightmares about how we were going to feed a baby while traveling through Asia, staying in places where sanitary conditions were definitely not up to my standards. I was so anxious about not being able to see where or how the food was prepared. How could I check that the surfaces and the utensils were clean, the ingredients were washed? I was convinced that Levi would get sick.

So I created an incorruptible, ideal meal: a combination of poached fish, brown rice, and seaweed. I cooked up batches of it before we left. I boiled the rice to death, at least three times, and then added the fish, which I had poached. I was completely paranoid about my young son choking on any fine fish bones, so I used a fish like halibut, which I deboned. I was so obsessed I think I even used tweezers! Then I cooked the seaweed, which has a nice delicate flavor, until it was soft. I didn't use any salt.

I combined the ingredients like congee, a traditional Chinese breakfast gruel.

Essentially, I created the ideal baby food!

I packed the little portions of congee in bags of ice in a carry-on cooler. We traveled across the ocean with our baby under one arm and that cooler in the other. In those years, you could carry anything onto a plane. Today, it would be a different scenario.

We arrived first in Bangkok. I had prepared enough baby food to last two weeks. Next, we traveled to Phuket, where we stayed at the original Amanpuri Resort. The hotel had the first infinity swimming pool that I had ever seen; I didn't realize that it wasn't a sheet of glass. My first impressions were of the incredible lushness of the vegetation and the gentle slapping of flip-flops on the paths: the sounds of relaxation.

At the resort, I bumped into one of my cooking friends, who used to own the Parrot restaurant in Toronto, not far from where I was working at the time, which was a restaurant called Peter Pan. Doug was hanging out at Amanpuri, having lunch! He had moved to Phuket and invited us to his house. His home was close to the water, and at low tide you could walk for miles. That memory of walking on the warm sand, under a hot sun, the Chinese junks floating silently on the horizon, the pungent smell in my nostrils of sun-dried fish — which they use for fermented fish paste — remains for me an indelible stamp of Thailand.

But back to my story. I didn't trust anyone to feed Levi except me. I admit that I'm a bit of a traditional Chinese father that way — he was the first male child and I was so protective, very controlling.

Since we were guests at the Amanpuri Resort, I figured it was all right to ask if I could go into the kitchen, to warm up Levi's baby food in a pot of water.

The entire staff in the hotel kitchen was female. I was surrounded by Thai ladies: the chef, sous-chefs, and assistant cooks. They were absolutely hospitable and helpful, even though I was an intruder who was interrupting their routine.

I remember that the smell of the ground chiles was so

powerful that I immediately started to sneeze. In the kitchen! I can't believe those ladies didn't toss me out the door. I peered over their shoulders and peeked into their pots, asking, "What's in this sauce? How did you make that paste?"

The environment of that kitchen was a revelation: pure stainless steel surfaces everywhere, balanced by the graceful rhythm of the women as they moved around and stirred their sauces, concentrating over their curry pastes, grinding their chiles. No yelling, no banging. No recipes written down. These women cooked with their hearts. I felt as though I was in someone's home. I was the only man in the hotel kitchen, and yet I immediately felt welcome. The women were eager to share with me — explaining the names of the local ingredients, their techniques, their recipes.

Because this was twenty years ago, the environment was a striking contrast to the kitchens in Malaysia and Indonesia, where the head chefs were all men. I realized at that moment one of the great gifts of Thai culture: the openness and lack of preconception about male/female roles, the open-minded acceptance of each individual. Later, when I was a chef at the Four Seasons and noticed a transvestite cook on the line, it was just business as usual.

The second day in Phuket I said to my wife, "I have to go

back into that kitchen." And so I did. My first exposure to Thai cuisine had been spontaneous and personally motivated, but the second time it was a deliberate, professional learning experience.

What fascinated me at Amanpuri was the culinary philosophy of creating the foundation of a dish from a curry paste. The experience in Phuket opened my mind: A paste could be the underlying architecture of flavor in a dish, but it could also be manipulated to achieve extraordinary effects with color.

In Thai cuisine, color signifies the vibrancy of a dish, and a Thai kitchen is like a paint shop: you can lay a foundation of primary tone, and mix from there. Green curry includes green chiles, turmeric, cumin, coriander, and fresh yellow ginger. Red chile pastes contain really red chilies, red tomatoes and red fruit.

My explorations at Amanpuri introduced me to the rainbow of colors and flavors of Thailand cuisine — lemongrass, peanut sauces, gingers. I discovered that there was blue ginger, white ginger, *and* yellow ginger. Thai cuisine also presented me with an amazing little root, *asam*, which has an almost indescribable taste; it's like a perfumed ginger, young and earthy. When ground, it becomes a paste with magical properties!

Those Amanpuri ladies didn't require written recipes for themselves, but they wrote them down for me, and taught me many valuable technical and cultural lessons about Thai cuisine. The influence of that exposure remains strong, and some of my most popular and acclaimed recipes were inspired by that visit into the hotel kitchen.

When I got back to Toronto, my head was spinning with ideas for new recipes based on my traveling adventures. Before I could throw anything into a pot and start experimenting, I had to do a lot of research: I needed to source which stores in my hometown could provide me with fresh spices. It was a stroke of luck to find a company not far from my restaurant that imported fresh ingredients. You better believe I treasured that supplier like gold.

Armed with my fresh spices, I decided to elaborate on the traditional Thai green curry that uses chicken or shrimp, replacing the chicken with lamb. My marinated rack of lamb, served with sides of eggplant and coriander tart and roasted polenta, became one of my signature dishes. I dubbed it, "Lamb Thailandaise."

The secret ingredient in this dish, which no one, not even my assistant chef, can replicate, is green curry. This much I will reveal: it contains three types of ginger, *asam* root, coriander, and fermented shrimp paste. However, nobody knows the proportions or the complete recipe but me, and it's hidden in my brain!

I consider my green curry to be the source of my Asian success. I'm using it at Club Chinois, my new restaurant in Singapore, and also in the menu at my restaurant Shang in Manhattan.

Funny to think that it all began by stepping across the threshold of the kitchen at the Amanpuri Resort in Phuket to warm up my baby son's ideal meal.

My son never did get sick in Thailand.

He's now twenty years old, and he's learning the ropes in the restaurant business. It just occurred to me that the next time he ticks me off, I could remind him that his dad went to some pretty extreme lengths on his behalf. I'm hoping that he'll read this story.

David Sax is the author of *Save the Deli: In Search of Perfect Pastrami, Crusty Rye, and the Heart of the Jewish Delicatessen,* which won the 2010 James Beard Foundation Award for Writing and Literature. Originally from Toronto, David lived for three years in both Buenos Aires, Argentina and Rio de Janeiro, Brazil, covering South American politics, business, travel, and culture for publications including the *Globe and Mail,* the *Walrus, Wine Spectator, Foreign Policy,* and the *New Republic* . . . not to mention a few surfing magazines. After returning to Canada he continued writing articles and his work has appeared in *New York Magazine, Saveur,* the *New York Times, Rolling Stone, GQ, American Way, The Huffington Post,* and on National Public Radio. He lives in Toronto with his wife, who prefers simple meals.

COOKING BY CABLE

David Sax

I'd begun the freshmen ski trip at McGill by slugging Jack Daniel's straight from the bottle, and ended up with the worst sore throat I'd ever experienced. Over the next few days, as my fever soared, the throat constricted further, so that I could barely swallow my precious chicken Caesar wraps. I tossed on my sweatpants, grabbed my backpack, and hopped a train back to mommy in Toronto. The doctor took one look at me and let me know I had mononucleosis, also known as mono or the "kissing disease" (unfortunately, I hadn't kissed anyone).

Mono is a funny sickness. After a week or so the sore throat subsides, and all you're really left with is a general fatigue. If you have to work, or are required to exert physical labor, it's quite debilitating. But if you're a freshman studying liberal arts, it's basically a four-week vacation with a license to watch as much television as possible. So I settled into the sectional sofa in my parents' basement, and surrendered to the cable box.

About a week in, I was flipping through the upper channels, and found a new face on the Canadian cable spectrum: the Food Network. Because the rest of daytime television was a morass of reruns and news talk, the Food Network offered something fresh every day. As a kid, I had always been drawn to cooking shows, sopping up the antics of Graham Kerr's *Galloping Gourmet,* giggling at the arias tossed out by the singing chef who hosted the public access show *Pasquale's Kitchen,* or taking delight in the slogans on Martin Yan's aprons on *Yan Can Cook.* My first attempt at cooking, when I was eleven, came after James Barber, host of *The Urban Peasant* on CBC, made something called banana chicken. I made my mom dig out an ancient box of cornstarch, and we set to work, ruining a perfectly good chicken and banana in the process.

Food wasn't really high on the curriculum during my first year at McGill University. In the freshman residences above campus, our meals were taken at a central cafeteria where the steam tray and deep fryer ruled the palate. The catering was done by the same outfit that took care of Canada's prisons, and the women who slopped out the portions with ice cream scoops did not mess around. This was institutional eating, straight from the freezer truck. Bread was white. Salads were iceberg. Joe's were sloppy. The culinary highlight of our week was chicken burgers: oil-scalded fried pucks of minced chicken cartilage . . . on a bun. I didn't care too much about eating, other than for pure sustenance, but all that changed with mono.

From morning until prime time I lay in front of a channel that would fill my days with recipes, ingredients, and inspiration. I fell into a rhythm with the schedule: *Molto Mario*, Sara Moulton's *Cooking Live*, *East Meets West with Ming Tsai*, *Grillin' & Chillin'* with Bobby Flay and Jack McDavid, *Two Fat Ladies*, and *The Naked Chef* with Jamie Oliver. It was great fun, but it didn't really propel me into the kitchen. Until I met him . . . my muse.

Emeril Lagasse had a daytime show called *Essence of Emeril,* in the same drab studio kitchen as the other chefs. He always seemed awkward, like his personality was stuffed into a shirt two sizes too small. You could tell this man wanted to say something, do something big, but he was alone out there, in front of the lights with nothing but his pans and spring-loaded tongs. His dishes — a mix of southern, Cajun, and Massachusetts Portuguese — were interesting, but didn't make me salivate. It was just one show out of many, and I paid it little mind.

Then, one night, I strayed back to the Food Network from a prime-time diet of *Seinfeld* reruns. There was Emeril, exploding into a mass of stocky energy on his other show, *Emeril Live*. Bongos and bass pumped from a house band. Lagasse ran around the set, slapping flesh and whipping a live studio audience into a frenzy like he was Bob Barker in chef's whites. This wasn't cooking. This was theater. This was chutzpah. I was fired up and he hadn't said a single word. He started making some chicken dish, tossing about the birds as casually as anything, then picked up a pinch of pepper, and "BAM!"

What the hell was that? It was like a shotgun blast. Again, he grabbed a pinch of salt, and "BAM!"

Quickly, I found myself a devoted follower in the church of Emeril. I learned the rhythm of the show, knowing when he'd give the shout out to Doc Gibbs, when he'd announce the recipe, when the knife would come out. Besides the fiery BAMming, there were sayings like "Kick it up a notch" and "Oh yeah, babe" that set the tone of the hour. And yet, amid all the shouting and antics, I began to absorb the substance behind Lagasse's showmanship.

I watched how he chopped garlic, smashing it first with the flat blade of the knife, then rocking the tip to mince it into a fine paste. I listened as he built a seasoning, layering the flavors throughout the cooking process, a bit at a time, rather than just salting at the end. I observed how Emeril cooked different vegetables at different times, taking into account their density, flavor profile, and moisture content, so he would end up with a dish that had consistent textures. I learned to sear, to grill, to braise, to properly boil. I got daily instruction in chopping, dicing, and slicing. I learned the vocabulary of classical cooking, all those French words for techniques, ingredients, and appliances that are essential to reading a recipe or shopping for ingredients.

"You should thicken that with a roux," I'd tell my perplexed mother, who was cooking upstairs. "You know, kick it up a notch."

Despite all the talk, I didn't actually cook much. My parents were home, and when I went back to school, it was chicken burgers all over again. Only when I moved into my first apartment the following fall did I get control of my own kitchen. I stocked it with all my parents' old dishware and utensils, and watched Emeril nightly, waiting for the right dish to test my skills. It came a week before Canadian Thanksgiving, in the form of turkey gumbo.

Here was a one-pot dish that looked simple, but required all the skills I'd learned: slicing, seasoning, searing, and braising. I went to the bookstore and bought a copy of *Emeril's New New Orleans Cooking*, which had the gumbo recipe. I drove across Montreal, looking for cayenne, the freshest vegetables, the Cajun andouille sausage that gave it the right kick. I cleaned our kitchen (a challenge in itself), skipped class, and spent eight hours prepping. I shredded the turkey meat, and boiled the bones for stock. I diced bell peppers, celery, and onions, chopped the sausage, and began building the stew, first with the roux, and then layering and seasoning gradually. While it simmered, I whipped out a newly acquired cast-iron skillet and made Emeril's cornbread, diced and seasoned a hoisin coleslaw from Ming Tsai, and sautéed some broccoli with crisp shallots from Jamie Oliver.

My roommates and I moved the table into the living room, set it with what passed as a clean sheet, and lit some Ikea votives. The girls who lived upstairs were invited over, and they brought a few bottles of Baby Duck (wine so cheap it opens with a pull tab), plus a real bottle of something crisp and white. We cobbled together desk chairs, mismatched cutlery, and paper towels, and I set the steaming cauldron of gumbo on the table. I ladled it into each bowl with such pride, watching as the first spoonfuls were cautiously taken to the mouth, examined, and consumed. Compliments abounded.

Laughter resumed. The Baby Duck flowed like only $5 wine can.

That meal was the first of many in that apartment, with Emeril and his cohorts guiding me nightly into becoming a competent home cook. I'd get home from class, catch a few episodes on the Food Network, and set about making some variation of that (sans truffle oil). My skills improved, a sense of taste emerged, and I soon abandoned recipes in favor of improvisation. Inevitably, the Food Network and I drifted apart. Emeril's antics became less interesting, especially once the spectacle of Japan's *Iron Chef* came along. New shows began focusing more on entertainment and less on technique, and after 9/11, I dropped the Food Network for BBC World News.

I haven't had cable TV since 2002, and rarely watch cooking shows, but every night when I enter the kitchen I know I have two beings to thank. The first is that over-the-top cook from New Orleans by way of the Food Network, who was the Julia Child of my own life. And the other is that cell of the mononucleosis virus that somehow got into my system without a single kiss at the right moment in the programming cycle. If I'd contracted mono today, I'd probably just watch *The Wire*.

Amy Sherman is a San Francisco–based food writer, recipe developer, and restaurant reviewer. She is author of *Williams-Sonoma New Flavors for Appetizers* and *WinePassport: Portugal,* and is the creator of the popular blog Cooking with Amy. She also writes for Epicurious.com and Frommers.com on culinary travel and for *Cheers* magazine about pairing wine, beer, and spirits with food.

THE MOST IMPORTANT
MEAL OF THE DAY

Amy Sherman

When I was growing up, I used to skip breakfast. I wasn't much of a morning person and I loved sleeping in. Basic breakfast food bored me and, for the most part, it still does. I remember going on road trips with my family and stopping at coffee shops or diners for breakfast. I would plead for an order of soup or chili and my sister would politely request a cheeseburger. Sadly, we were generally limited to breakfast items because lunch was not served until, you know, lunch. I went through phases where I refused to eat pancakes and just the smell of maple syrup sent me backing out of the dining room in disgust.

It seems that breakfast is an easy meal to ruin. Everyone I know is fussy about how they like their eggs, and at one time or another we've all had terrible French toast that was dry in the middle or pancakes tinged with too much baking powder. Truly great breakfast spots inevitably have lines out the door, especially on the weekends when we all deserve a bit of pampering. Standing on line is not my idea of a good breakfast appetizer!

In part because I am the one cooking, my favorite breakfasts at home are generally leftovers from the night before. Reheated pasta or pizza with or without an egg on top makes me happy first thing in the morning. But that's not my husband Lee's favored breakfast fare. When we were first dating we talked about meals constantly and he always wanted to know what I would cook for breakfast. He loves a traditional breakfast and so it seems I have warmed up to it as well or at the very least to cooking it.

In the years since we have been together the morning has always included "tea with the love." Apparently if I make the tea and serve it to him, it tastes different than if he makes it for himself. Who knew? When I was single, the idea of serving my partner tea every morning would have bothered me on a number of levels, but now to be able to give the person I love such a simple joy is a pleasure.

Our wedding was held in the morning, and the meal we served to our guests was brunch. No rubber chicken dinner! I figured a hotel kitchen could not mess up brunch fare — we dined on crisp hot waffles, delicate smoked salmon with all the trimmings, eggs Florentine, bacon, sausages, and a myriad of pastries, all washed down with fresh juices and Champagne.

Since we've been married, we go out for breakfast now and again, and our vacations always include an effort to find the most interesting breakfasts possible. We have had memorable morning noodle soups in Vietnam, breakfast extravaganzas at Hugo's in West Hollywood (where the menu goes on for pages), and the best French toast of my life at Veritable Quandry in Portland, Oregon. Recently, we had an amazing breakfast in Santa Cruz at Café Brasil, where the banana pancakes reminded me of the ones I ate in college, and spicy concoctions of eggs, beans, salsa, avocado, and cheese were robust and filling. In New York, breakfast with relatives always seems to be bagels or bialys, salty lox, and cream cheese.

In San Francisco our favorite breakfast destination is Pastores Restaurant, but we call it "Irma's" after the proprietor and chef, who is our de facto Mexican mamacita. She makes luscious chilaquiles with piquant green sauce and fried eggs for Lee and for me an order of chicken mole enchiladas, served with beans, rice, and tortillas. Her food is so soul-satisfying that it can make up for any physical or emotional pains conceivable.

Enchiladas may not be a classic breakfast food, but I firmly believe you should eat whatever makes you happy.

At home I make elaborate breakfasts on the weekends, featuring dishes like eggs Benedict, fruit stuffed crepes, and Lee's favorite, Dutch baby. The recipe for the Dutch baby comes from an old issue of *Sunset* magazine that I tweaked slightly. I make it in a small, enameled cast-iron skillet that has long been without a wooden handle. I have two of these pans that were handed down from my parents and they are treasured possessions. First of all, they are indestructible, but also they remind me of my childhood home and the mornings my father lovingly fried up leftover potatoes for me.

I turn the oven as high as it will go to thoroughly heat the pan. I add a thick pat of butter and if it sizzles I know the pan is hot enough. The batter is easy as can be; it's one egg, one egg white, ¼ cup of all-purpose flour, and ¼ cup of milk. I can whisk it together or whip it up in the blender, either way with a touch of salt. It spills into the pan and back into the oven it goes. That's where the alchemy happens. A hot pan transforms an eggy batter into a crisp-on-the-outside and soft-on-the-inside bowl-shaped puffed pancake. After fifteen minutes or so in the oven it slips easily out of the pan, never sticking one bit. It's a recipe I make by feel, not looking at the clock or setting the oven to a precise temperature.

The Dutch baby can be filled with a dollop of yogurt and sliced fruit such as bananas, mangoes, peaches, strawberries, blueberries, or Lee's favorite, kiwi fruit. Or you can serve it with fresh-squeezed lemon and powdered sugar. A side of bacon or sausage allows you to enjoy both savory and sweet in one meal.

Breakfast is literally breaking a fast. Waking up, getting up but then settling back down at the table to eat and drink and/or read or, best of all, chat. While the evening meal is often the culmination of the day, in the morning the day is filled with potential. Bodies and minds are just beginning to stir instead of winding down. It's a time to make plans, to dream of what the day will bring, and gently ease into the flow. It's a precious time no matter what you like to eat.

Jansen Chan, executive pastry chef of Oceana in New York City, has been indulging diners with his sumptuous and visually arresting desserts and artisanal breads. After completing his architecture degree at the University of California, Berkeley, Jansen attended Le Cordon Bleu in Paris. He has worked at Fifth Floor in San Francisco, Mix in Las Vegas, and Alain Ducasse at the Essex House in New York City. His desserts have been featured in *Food & Wine* and on the Food Network, and were declared "splendid" and "a delight of flavors" by the *New York Times*.

A SWEET END

Jansen Chan

The "perfect meal" immediately conjures up so many images: golden stuffed birds, glazed fork-tender meats adorned with slow-roasted, vegetables and a rich jus, succulent prime rib with soft, creamy mashed potatoes, or moist, dense lasagna with countless layers of pasta and sauce made from a grandmother's secret Italian recipe passed from generation to generation. There are so many alternate paradises in the universe of food. The visions are endless and sublime. Choosing one is incredible and unfair but it's still a joy to imagine.

My culinary experiences range from a nineteen-course tasting feast at New York City's finest restaurant to a banquet of Chinese dishes cooked by own mother. Plus, I have had the unique opportunity to have worked with and tasted the food of some of the world's best chefs — I even cooked for America's beloved Julia Child for her ninetieth birthday bash in San Francisco. But my personal list of what constitutes a "perfect meal" varies as much as the collective body of a New York subway car. I'm a Chinese-American pastry chef who eats every ethnic food on the island of Manhattan (and even in a borough across a bridge.) There are few limits to my personal culinary delights and, hopefully, I will never have to narrow the borders of joyful experimentation.

To save myself from this nearly impossible task of selecting dishes for my perfect meal, I will focus instead on the one part that matters most: the end. Of course, every perfect meal must reach a conclusion and for most people that would be the sweet finale of dessert. Enter visions of frosted layered cakes; creamy, silky puddings; cookies in a rainbow's color; fresh fruit pies; and other favorites. Think of ice creams and sorbets melting into hot, cloudlike soufflés or steamy, molten chocolate cakes. Swirl around the world and find custard-filled French eclairs, fresh and light New Zealand pavlovas, and sticky, decadent, nut-filled Greek baklavas. The task here is not any easier but this is my domain. This is my livelihood.

I have always loved "the process." Perhaps that is why being a pastry chef is the perfect profession for me. There is a clear and distinct order that needs to be adhered to so that the daily operational tasks are executed successfully. Bread-making is a set schedule. Feed the starter, mix the dough, proof, shape, proof, bake with steam, bake without steam, and so forth. The order is logical, practical, and functional. It is the science of pastry. Much like any physical or chemical law, it has to be obeyed and respected. Simply put, you can't frost the cake before you bake the cake.

But beyond the process is the artistry. The artistry is what differentiates one chef from another. It's how you earn a gold medal for figure skating at the Olympics. It's why the Eiffel Tower is the icon of architectural engineering. Creating beyond the standard is the test of any good pastry chef. It took many years to learn that valuable lesson.

The most interesting thing I've learned about serving desserts is that people have clear expectations about what constitutes a satisfying experience. They have such a strong memory of desserts they've enjoyed and seemingly need to connect the current experience to their past. So many times customers have told me about a pie or cake they had somewhere else in their lives and asked if I had the knowledge to recreate it. Sadly, I often smile and tell them yes, but I sensed inwardly that I probably couldn't live up to their expectations to capture that moment in time. It wasn't due to lack of ability or knowledge, but rather an inability to recreate the perfect components of environment, ingredients, and mindset. It's all those elements that make up lasting food memories. I find it a risky proposition to tackle such a nestled memory. I know that this beyond my job description.

It is safer to create a new standard with my own desserts. Take the current or old and recreate it in a way that is visually memorable and taste-defining. Basics are great but I want a challenge. Each dish I develop is a reflection of me, my attitude, my history, my technical ability, and some great ingredients.

I was asked to recreate some classic Chinese sweets for an event celebrating the newly built Museum of Chinese America (MOCA) in New York City. Since I'm of Chinese descent, this may have appeared to be an easy assignment, but the task was tricky. First, there are no traditional Chinese desserts, but rather collective sweets that are served normally throughout the day, or at special festivals and holidays. The western model of a dessert course is typically replaced by a dish of freshly cut seasonal fruits, such as oranges or lichees. Second, I needed to stay away from the obvious solution of taking a traditional Asian ingredient and placing it in a classic French-style pastry. No need for a green tea crème brûlée or a red bean paste cupcake. Many "fusion" style restaurants fail horribly at this approach. Using an Asian flavor in a dish does not constitute the merging of two cultures. The best way to achieve such fusion is through the understanding of different cooking techniques and the melding of them, while respecting each one's unique regional heritage.

Dessert preferences vary. Of course, in Asia, where sweets are not bound to the end of the meal, the expectation is usually that they'll be sweeter and less rich. In Europe, the opposite is true. And in America, the sweets run sweeter and richer. God bless the Twinkie. Understanding a middle ground in this melting pot of cultures and ideas is important for the modern chef.

For my MOCA mission, I chose to focus on a classic dim sum treat: steamed golden cake. It is a childhood favorite, simple and clean and served silently in countless Chinese bakeries. Although really just a snack and not designed to be a formal dessert, I knew this simple cake could be transformed to be a stand-alone treat for even the most finicky diners.

The road to success for this dessert is the steaming of the cake. It is this distinct technique that produces an unusually moist yet dry texture. Eggs and sugar are whipped until they are virtually all foam, and welded together by the smallest amount of wheat flour. No additional fat, which usually yields more flavor and tenderness, is added. In updating this classic, I knew the easiest (and tastiest) way to add some of the fat was to make it a chocolate steamed cake. By adding cocoa fat and the dark bitter cocoa, the steamed cakes were transformed to rich, flavorful bites of bliss, while still maintaining the original strong, dense sponge texture. Still not satisfied, I knew that to counter the monotonous nature of the cake I was going to need to produce a new element.

The visual of a dessert is the selling point. Pastry is a luxury — an everyperson's affordable treat. It's not a necessity of life. We could avoid sweets our whole lives and function perfectly fine. But it is the eye-catching appeal that triggers our taste buds and memories. For the chocolate cake, I felt I needed a hook. Drawing from my classic European training, I decided to add French pastry cream — a fairly standard, basic building block of eggs, milk, sugar, and starch. But instead of the common vanilla-flavored cream, I reconnected this tea-time snack to its roots by introducing green jasmine tea. So, buried deep inside the tender cocoa cake I placed a cavern of creamy, warm jasmine-infused custard that oozed out when taking that first bite. This was the exact element I needed: a new texture, a new, bright aromatic flavor, and the "wow" factor. Once I figured out the physics of steaming the cake while containing the loose custard center set inside, I knew I had the perfect dish.

Indeed, the dessert was a hit. Each precious cake was about the size of the average cupcake. Set in carefully cut parchment rings with over-exaggerated tall edges and dusted generously with powdered sugar to counter the dark exterior of the cake, the new chocolate sponge cake had all the familiar trappings of its predecessor but a whole new slew of flavors and textures. Still incredibly moist and tender, the cocoa batter — baked with little chocolate chips melted in — gave way to the smooth, sweet custard, as if frosted from the inside out. And, of course, the first taste of the custard reveals a pleasant surprise, the recognizable flavor of spring jasmine tea. The tea and chocolate are a marriage of flavors bringing their vastly different histories into one product. The bittersweet cocoa is complemented by the floral scents of the jasmine leaves.

In all honesty, the steamed chocolate jasmine cake would not be the only dessert at the end of my "perfect meal." In fact, it would be part of a mini-meal, or a tasting of desserts. I would need to quench my endless palate with fresh, seasonal fruits; flaky, buttery crusts; and creamy mousses sandwiched with crisp, sugary cookies. However, that cake represents perfection in itself: the merging of skills, cultures, and physical pastry laws. I nurtured the process that went into its creation and ended up creating a new version of one of my favorite childhood sweets. And, most importantly, it tasted pretty darn good.

STEAMED CHOCOLATE JASMINE CAKES   *Serves 15*

CHOCOLATE CAKE BATTER

1¼ cups cake flour

¼ cup unsweetened natural cocoa powder

½ teaspoon salt

¼ teaspoon baking soda

¼ teaspoon baking powder

6 large eggs, separated

1¼ cups firmly packed dark brown sugar

1 tablespoon brewed cold espresso (strong cold coffee will work, too)

¼ cup butter, melted

1 cup chopped chocolate chips (55% cacao)

For the cake batter: In a medium bowl, sift together the flour, cocoa, salt, baking soda, and baking powder. In a large bowl with an electric mixer, whip the egg yolks to a thick ribbon consistency with ½ cup plus 2 tablespoons of the brown sugar. Add the espresso. Wash and dry the beaters.

In another large, clean bowl, slowly whip the egg whites until foamy, soft peaks form. Increase the speed, then slowly add the remaining brown sugar, and whip until stiff peaks form.

Begin folding some of the dry ingredients into the yolk mixture. Alternate with the whipped whites. Toward the end of the folding process, add a little batter to the melted butter and whisk until smooth. Add the butter to the batter, along with the chocolate, and fold until well mixed.

JASMINE CUSTARD

2½ cups milk

15 grams loose jasmine tea (or 7 tea bags)

¼ cup granulated sugar, split

3 large egg yolks

2 teaspoons cornstarch

¼ cup butter

Confectioners' sugar for serving

For the jasmine custard: Bring the milk to a boil in a medium pot. Turn off the heat, add the tea, cover, and let steep for 3 minutes. Strain, or remove the tea bags. Remeasure 2 cups of tea milk. Discard the remainder. Bring the 2 cups of tea milk to a boil with 2 tablespoons of the granulated sugar. Meanwhile, whisk together the egg yolks and remaining 2 tablespoons sugar, then whisk in the cornstarch. Pour a little of the hot tea milk into the yolk mixture, whisking constantly to raise the temperature. Return the yolk mixture to the pot and whisk over medium heat until boiling. Continue whisking for 2 minutes at a slow boil. Remove from the heat, let cool briefly, and place plastic wrap directly on the surface. (This will keep a skin from forming.) When barely warm, whisk in the butter. Cover with plastic wrap directly on the surface again and let chill.

To steam: Prepare a bamboo steamer over simmering water. For a make-shift steamer, use a large pot, with an inch of simmering water that can accommodate an elevated muffin tin (or 4-ounce ring molds) and a tight, fitted lid. Spray the muffin tin with nonstick cooking spray. If you use ring molds, line the side and bottom with parchment paper and coat with cooking spray. Fill molds with batter two-thirds of the way up. Place about 1 tablespoon of the chilled jasmine custard filling in the center of the chocolate batter. Cover the top with a little more batter. Place on the steamer rack and cover the steamer. Steam until there is a light spring in the center of the cake when touched, 14 to 15 minutes.

The cakes should be cooled in the rings for at least 10 minutes before removing. Let cakes cool completely. Wrap in plastic wrap until needed to retain moisture. The cakes should be made the same day but, if necessary, can be refrigerated overnight in plastic wrap. Serve at room temperature.

Before serving, dust generously with confectioners' sugar.

Mary Ann Esposito is the creator and host of the nationally broadcast PBS series *Ciao Italia,* now in its twenty-first year, making it the longest-running cooking series on public television. Mary Ann holds a masters degree in food history from the University of New Hampshire; her thesis work was on Renaissance Italian foods. She also holds an honorary doctorate degree in Humane Letters from St. Anselm College in Manchester, N.H. Mary Ann is the author of eleven cookbooks, including *Ciao Italia: Five-Ingredient Favorites.* Mary Ann has appeared as a guest chef on the *Today Show, Regis and Kathy Lee,* and on Discovery, the Food Network, QVC, Fox, Pax, Martha Stewart Radio, and a host of others. She has been featured in print in newspapers and magazines, including *TV Guide, People Magazine. Family Circle, Yankee,* and *USA Today.* She has been honored by numerous organizations for her work in preserving traditional Italian foods and culture.

DINNER WITH THE BARONE
AND THE BARONESSA

Mary Ann Esposito

I am the first one to admit that I live in the past when it comes to cooking. Tradition means a lot to me and over the years on the television series *Ciao Italia,* I have showcased the home cooking *(casalinga)* of my mother and grandmothers. Their "recipes," based on ingenuity, have been my building blocks, since much of what I do comes from their Southern Italian roots and what I observe whenever I am in Italy. I am always looking for those traditional dishes that are in danger of disappearing.

So when I was invited by a dear Sicilian friend to dinner at the baroque palazzo of the Barone Rocco and Baronessa Luisa Garofalo Camerata in Palermo, I knew that the evening would be very special. Just the thought of dining in a palazzo brought mental images of feasting like Don Fabrizio Corbero, the Prince of Salina and main character in the classic book

The Leopard, a tale of the fading Sicilian aristocracy in the late-nineteenth century where the imagery of aristocratic foods are vividly described and the reader questions whether anyone really ate that way.

We arrived punctually and were greeted at the gargantuan wooden door, etched with the baron's coat of arms, by a doorman dressed in a Wedgewood blue uniform trimmed with gold buttons. His white-gloved hands waved us into a foyer decorated with fourteenth-century ancestral paintings and antique gilded furniture. It would be no ordinary evening.

After pleasantries were exchanged and we nibbled on traditional antipasti of *panelle* (chickpea fritters), tuna pâté on crackers, and *arancine* (little fried rice balls), we were escorted into the opulent dining room with a long dining table that could seat twenty-five. In the center a long mirrored tray held gorgeous pink and white flowers under a magnificent chandelier. The baron sat at one end of the table and the baronessa at the other. I sat next to her, which was delightful because I came to find out that she loved to cook too! We talked about the many ways to make *caponata*, an eggplant relish that is one of the hallmarks of Sicilian cooking with its *agrodolce* (sweet and sour) taste. There are many versions she said, some with pistachio nuts, some with smoked swordfish or octopus.

As we talked, a slow and seemingly unending parade of foods arrived, including fusilli with anchovy and tomato sauce, small bundles of veal housing caciocavallo cheese and pine nuts, and grilled swordfish with raisins, citron, and tiny potatoes. These were classics and, I surmised, ones that Don Fabrizio would have enjoyed. The highlight was the *timballo*, an impressive drum of glazed-looking eggplant encasing cheese, tiny meatballs, and bucatini, all enveloped in rich tomato sauce. It arrived in all its glory on a large silver tray; savory smells wafted like a genie and hit the senses as soon as it was cut before us into thick wedges. It was opulent in its commonality of ingredients — eggplant, tomatoes, cheese — local ingredients that told the story of Sicily's culinary heritage on a plate. One forkful told me that this was the dish that I must have again and again. I savored every bite, reconstructing in my mind its complexity of flavors. If only I could jot down the ingredients . . .

Dessert and coffee were offered in the drawing room. The smoothest vanilla-scented semifreddo, served on a puddle of bitter orange sauce with chunks of blood oranges, was as close to a culinary victory as Garibaldi's unification of Italy.

Toasts of "Cin cin" with Marsala wine ("May you live a hundred years") to the baron and baronessa and I knew that as soon as I arrived back home, I would be recreating from memory that *timballo* and at the same time preserving the past for the present.

TIMBALLO DI MELANZANE E BUCATINI
(EGGPLANT AND BUCATINI CASSEROLE)   *Serves 10-12*

4 tablespoons olive oil

½ cup toasted breadcrumbs

3 eggplant at least 11 inches long, cut into ¼-inch-thick lengthwise slices

SAUCE

2 tablespoons olive oil

½ cup minced onions

1 rib celery, minced

1 large carrot, scraped and minced

2 cloves garlic, minced

5 cups chopped fresh or canned plum tomatoes

¼ cup dry red wine

1 bay leaf

Salt and freshly ground black pepper

FILLING

1 pound ground veal

1 large egg, lightly beaten

2 tablespoons dry white wine

6 tablespoons grated pecorino cheese

½ cup fresh breadcrumbs

1 teaspoon salt

2 cups cooked bucatini or spaghetti, broken into thirds

1½ cups fresh mozzarella cheese cut into bits

¼ cup minced fresh Italian parsley

Use 1 tablespoon of the olive oil to grease a 10 x 3-inch-deep spring-form pan. Coat it with toasted breadcrumbs and place in the refrigerator (do this a day ahead).

Preheat the oven to 350°F

Brush two or three baking sheets with the remaining 3 tablespoons olive oil and lay the eggplant slices on them in a single layer. Bake the slices in batches, until they begin to brown, 5 to 7 minutes; they should be soft and pliable, not mushy. Cool the slices.

For the sauce: Heat the olive oil in a large saucepan over medium heat. Add the onions, celery, and carrot. Cook, stirring occasionally, until the vegetables soften. Stir in the garlic and cook until it begins to soften. Stir in the tomatoes, wine, and bay leaf. Cover the pan. Lower the heat to medium low and cook for 20 minutes.

Remove the cover and simmer the sauce for 5 minutes. Season with salt and freshly ground black pepper. Set aside. (This step can be done weeks ahead and the sauce frozen or made 3 or 4 days ahead.)

For the filling: If necessary, preheat the oven to 350°F.

Combine the veal, egg, wine, 2 tablespoons of the pecorino, the fresh breadcrumbs, and salt in a medium bowl. Mix just to combine the ingredients. Wet your hands and make marble-size meatballs. Place them on a rimmed baking sheet and bake until cooked through, 7 to 10 minutes. Transfer the meatballs to a large bowl. (This can be done 2 days ahead and refrigerated).

Line and overlap the baked eggplant slices lengthwise over the sides of the prepared springform pan, leaving about a 3-inch overhang. Do not leave any gaps around the edge of the pan. Line the base of the pan with more slices, and be sure to fill in any gaps with smaller pieces of eggplant.

Add the bucatini to the same bowl as the meatballs. Stir in 2 cups of the sauce and the mozzarella. Combine the mixture well. Spoon the mixture into the pan, packing it in tightly.

Fold the overlapping ends of the eggplant slices in towards the center of the pan, covering the ingredients. Place the pan on a rimmed baking sheet to catch any drips.

Spread ½ cup of sauce over the top of the mold and sprinkle with the remaining 4 tablespoons pecorino. Cover the top tightly with a sheet of aluminum foil and bake for 45 minutes in a preheated 350°F oven. Uncover the pan and bake an additional 15 minutes.

Remove the pan from the oven and allow to rest tented with foil for 10 to 15 minutes to allow it to firm up before cutting into it.

Run a butter knife along the inside edge of the pan. Release the spring and place the *timballo* on a flat serving dish. Cut into wedges to serve with additional warm sauce on the side.

Tip: A neater cut will be achieved if the casserole is baked and refrigerated a day ahead. When ready to serve, reheat the casserole at 350°F, covered on a baking sheet, until it is hot, about 30 minutes, then remove from the oven; let rest for 5 minutes. Release the spring and remove the pan sides. Place the *timballo* on a serving dish; cut into thick wedges and serve with additional tomato sauce on the side.

Recipe for Timballo di Melanzine e Bucatini from *Ciao Italia Slow and Easy* by Mary Ann Esposito, © 2007 by the author and reprinted by permission of St. Martin's Press, LLC.

Mimi Sheraton is a pioneering food writer and former restaurant critic for *Cue,* the *Village Voice,* and the *New York Times.* Her writing on food and travel has appeared in such magazines as *Time, The New Yorker, Vogue, Town & Country, Mademoiselle, New York,* and *Food & Wine.* She has written sixteen books, including *The German Cookbook,* first published in 1975 and still in print, and a memoir, *Eating My Words: An Appetite for Life.* Her book *The Whole World Loves Chicken Soup* won both IACP and James Beard Foundation awards, and she won a James Beard Journalism Award for her article on the Four Seasons' fortieth anniversary in *Vanity Fair.*

FOR OLD TIME'S SAKE

Mimi Sheraton

Each year when particular holidays roll around, food writers, both in print and on the Web, provide recipes "for something different," inventive dishes as diversions from "the same old thing." Whether for Thanksgiving, Passover, Chanukah, Easter, or the Fourth of July, the "somethings different" usually suit the theme of the holiday, but not with what many regard as tiresome clichés.

Many, but not me. The once-a-year appearance of symbolic dishes is hardly frequent enough for them to become tiresome and, even more, in a world where few things remain constant, the annual roll-around of certain foods that always look and taste the same reassures the spirit and defines memories, especially for children. I even remember the warm and welcoming aromas that arose from the kitchen when my mother prepared a Passover Seder meal of dill-scented chicken soup, the wine-and-cinnamon-perfumed apple and walnut *charoses,* the oniony brisket, and the pungent wafts of hot sugar and orange announcing a baking sponge cake.

I realized the importance of this sort of gastronomic consistency the hard way when once, instead of turkey for Thanksgiving, I roasted a suckling pig, apple in the mouth and all. Not only was that a far more expensive and troublesome alternative, but, to my surprise, most guests smiled politely if wanly, a few muttering only half-jokingly that without turkey it did not feel like Thanksgiving. Two children cried. That piglet was too much for them.

Since then, the meals I have come to enjoy preparing most are the exact replicas of those that certain guests have loved, whether traditional for official holidays, or traditions I have established on my own. There is even a certain comfort and satisfaction in the rituals of preparation, rounding up the same utensils and going through the familiar motions as though performing a spiritual rite, with the prayer that I will arrive at what seems to be the exact same foods in the exact same serving dishes.

That brings me to one of my favorite holiday meals, to which I invite guests (mostly the same ones) every Fourth of July: a cookout in my garden, the small but verdant mini-jungle behind my Greenwich Village townhouse. At that season we enjoy an abundance of bright blue hydrangeas, lavender roses of Sharon, tumbles of purple and white petunias, and a dozen or so potfuls of herbs. My husband presides over the Weber for a cookout of moderate ambitions suited in scale to the moderate surroundings, local etiquette demanding that one refrain from activities that spill over into neighboring yards with sounds, scents, smoke, or, worst of all, flames.

And so we begin with deviled eggs made with Hellmann's® mayonnaise, ordinary prepared mustard, and a final flourish of paprika on top for a sunny, cheerful look. At other times I might fold chopped chives or truffles into the yolks or add a pinch of curry powder, but not for our country's birthday. A latter-day assimilated American addition among appetizers is guacamole and taco chips, without which our Independence no longer can be properly acknowledged.

For the main course, what else but hot dogs and hamburgers slipped into the best versions of the traditional buns that I can find? The hot dogs must be peppery and garlicky all-beef kosher-style in natural casings, as they are at the famed Katz's Delicatessen on Manhattan's Lower East Side, which is where we get them, along with uncooked sauerkraut that I simmer, plenty of cheap, sharp, and brassy mustard, and buns that will be lightly toasted on the grill. Garlic dill pickles are on my menu too, but homemade by me and put up ten days before the party so they will achieve full sourness, the only way I consider them to be true pickles. Our beefy hamburgers, formed of combined chuck and sirloin ground together, are *echte*, not thin patties, and have only salt and pepper for seasoning and round buns that also get a burnishing on the grill. Heinz® ketchup is the essential garnish, along with a platter of sliced, ripe red tomatoes and thin ringlets of sweet, raw red onions.

Of course, there's cole slaw, too — salt-wilted, chopped green cabbage with confetti flecks of carrot and green pepper and dill seed in a sweet-sour vinegar dressing — and German-style potato salad, unless we have decided to wrap potatoes in foil and do them mickey-style, roasting them under the grill's hot ashes to be served with lots of butter and coarse salt. In the past few years a new menu item has earned a place at our table: delectably soft and smoky, baked bronze kidney beans flecked with barbecue trimmings, something I buy at a nearby barbecue joint named RUB, as I cannot improve upon them myself.

All of this requires thirst quenchers and ours include iced beer, red wine, or iced tea with mint from the garden. Oddly, no cola drinks have ever been called for.

I take the simplest way out for dessert: a big bowl of the season's biggest, reddest cherries or some icy chunks of watermelon plus chocolate-covered vanilla Häagen-Dazs® ice cream pops for all. Come to think of it, maybe this year we'll do some toasted marshmallows for a final patriotic touch.

If guests and I love the simple directness of that July 4th menu, so do we cherish a far more complex Scandinavian smörgåsbord that my husband and I have done for the past twenty years when about seventy-five guests wander in and out of our home for a New Year's Day open house. It is largely a personal tradition recalling the pre-food period in my life during the 1950s when I wrote about furniture and interior design. Scandinavian modern was in vogue then and so I visited the four Nordic countries about three times a year. I developed a love of their food with its clean, fresh-air flavors and collected cookbooks, special utensils, and recipes from friends and chefs, and mastered the dishes back home. As one regular at our New Year's Day celebration puts it, "No matter what happens all year long, I know the gravlax will be fanned out on the same crystal platter, front and center on the dining table, with the dill mustard to the right and the thin, dark Danish rye bread on the left."

And so she can also feel safe about the rest, beginning with empty plates and forks (no knives needed) to be picked up and filled with, in this order: rosy beet, herring, and apple salad;

dilled shrimp and halibut salad; the Danes' beloved "Italian salad" with its cauliflower, carrots, and peas in a tarragon-flavored mousseline dressing; the silky coral gravlax that I cure; caraway and blue cheeses; wheaty Scandinavian crisp breads; tiny Swedish meatballs in cream gravy; the Danish-cured rolled and spiced meat that is *rullepølse*; baked Swedish brown beans with salt pork; and baked ham that, along with dessert cookies, are the only things I do not prepare myself.

Part of the fun for me is rounding up the authentic ingredients, such as the brown beans and sugar syrup from a Scandinavian shop in Connecticut, and digging out the *rullepølse* mold I bought about forty years ago in Copenhagen.

The rest of the fun is, naturally, seeing the same dear old faces looking happy and content as they stand in the same places, talking to the same people that they did the year before. I only hope they can do the same for many January firsts to come…

Jaden Hair is a television chef, food columnist, and award-winning food blogger at Steamy Kitchen.com. You can watch her cook twice a month on the syndicated *Daytime Show.* Jaden is a weekly food columnist for Discovery's TLC and for the *Tampa Tribune.* *The Steamy Kitchen Cookbook,* with 120 easy Asian recipes and over 200 color photographs, was published in 2009. Jaden has been featured on the *Today Show, CBS Early Show,* Martha Stewart Living Radio, Oprah.com, and in *Parents* magazine. In addition, she was recently named one of the "hottest women in food" and Forbes.com called her one of the best food bloggers. She is the mom of two little boys, Andrew and Nathan, who love to eat almost as much as she does!

A HIGH-STAKES GAME
OF HOT POT

Jaden Hair

Chinese fondue is called "hot pot" — and appropriately so. To me, love is laughter and when hot pot is involved, there's sure to be plenty of it. If you think playing a board game with your friends and family involves a high-stakes game of wit, just wait until you're around my family for hot pot. A large, wide pot of bubbly, boiling broth sits on a portable butane burner in the middle of a round dining table (round is best, so everyone is the same distance from the pot, with equal access to it) and jam-packed around the table are palm-sized dishes of every type of seafood, vegetable, and meat you can imagine, ready to cook. All the ingredients, from fresh fish, scallops, and clams to paper-thin sliced lamb, pork, and beef are all cut into bite-sized pieces that can cook in a flash, sometimes with just a fifteen-second swirl in the boiling broth.

Each person is armed with a pair of chopsticks, a little basket for cooking, and assorted dipping sauces. The wire basket has quite a lot of character — its long, skinny, twisted handle leads to a delicate cup-shaped vessel, deep enough to hold a whole egg comfortably. You pick and choose the ingredients that go into your little basket. A snap pea, rock shrimp, and maybe a bay scallop can fit in one go. Lower the basket into the hot pot and wait anywhere from a few seconds to a couple of minutes for it to cook. The basket handle is malleable and bendable, which is important. Bend the handle into a hook-shape to fit the shape of the pot's edge, sort of like an anchor, so that your hands are free to eat the previous batch that's cooling on your plate.

And this is where the fun begins.

As my family sits around the table, my brother Jay, who is always hungry and eager, is the first to call his territory in the pot. He fills his basket with meat, submerges it in the hot broth, cricks the handle, and lets it hang on the edge. That's one side. He then grabs his chopsticks, spears the scallop, and lets it cook about two inches away from the basket. The space that extends from the pie-shaped wedge right in front of him to the area in the hot pot between the basket and the chopsticks belongs him. That's his way of marking his territory.

Now, Mom, Dad, my husband, Scott, and I try to do the same thing. As the last person, I have to wedge my way in to claim some little spot in the pot. It may seem like I have the least advantage, but it always turns out that being the last is the smartest position to have. Without a basket to watch over (to ensure the meat doesn't overcook), I'm free to use nimble chopsticks and quick eyes to snag, steal, and swim for stray nuggets of food that have floated free from the baskets, especially from Scott, who seems to always overfill his basket.

The problem is, these very light baskets have no lid and when you try to submerge the thing in wildly bubbly, boiling broth, it ends up bobbing recklessly this way and that. Which is why the crick in the handle is important to latch onto the edge, though most of the time it proves ineffective.

There's nothing more disappointing than lifting up my basket that once held a full catch, only to have it come up with barely a scrap that resembles nibbled bait, while my husband next to me snickers in delight.

The quiet and calculating game of "You snatch mine, I'll snatch yours" ensues, which quickly escalates into downright plucking of a perfectly cooked clam right from someone's chopsticks just milliseconds before it reaches their lips.

Soon enough, the entire family bursts into fits of giggles, and in the end we all ditch the individual baskets and just dump the entire batch of food in the pot to share, family-style. Now that is a meal we all love.

Chef and cookbook author **Leticia Moreinos Schwartz** was born and raised in Rio de Janeiro, Brazil. After earning a B.A. in economics and working in finance, she changed careers and chose to follow her dreams. She moved to New York City in 1997 and enrolled at the French Culinary Institute, where she graduated with degrees in both Culinary and Pastry Arts. She cooked at such legendary New York restaurants as Le Cirque 2000, La Grenouille, La Caravelle, and Payard Patisserie & Bistro. She teaches at many New York cooking schools and is the author of *The Brazilian Kitchen: 100 Classic and Contemporary Recipes for the Home Cook.*

IT ALL ENDS IN SAMBA

Leticia Moreinos Schwartz

I cook almost every night and on some of those nights the dishes I make transport me to fabulous countries and cultures. For me, that is the secret of creating a meal you'll love.

But hey, who has time to travel every night? In our digitally driven era and stressful lives, aren't thirty-minute meals what people want most of the time? That's what we're often told, but when I feel like traveling, I know I look for exactly the opposite. The longer a meal takes to be prepared, the more I can explore the sights and sounds of a particular place — the main thoroughfares as well as the paths that are off-the-beaten track — which explains why I often choose menus that take hours, even days of preparation. The decision-making process can start at the farmer's market or on a morning while I browse the pages of one of my most precious possessions: my cookbook collection. Then I decide where I'll be traveling for the next two days. Depending on the country, the power of cooking might even trigger my polyglot side, even if I don't attempt more than just a few words of another language.

I have traveled extensively in my kitchen; I've been to Italy a gazillion times. *Ma que? Ai que buonissimo, me vollo piu,* I tell myself as I often go for seconds (I mix some Spanish with the few words I know in Italian). I cannot even tell you how many times I've been to France, *bien sûre. Et ici j'adore parler beaucoup, je ne ferme pas ma bouche.* Spain? *Riquíssimo, muchas vezes.* I love going to India and sometimes to China, where, er . . . well, I let my children do the talking for me there.

My favorite place in the whole wide world is my native country, Brazil, which allows me to think and speak, even sing in Portuguese, to the beautiful sound of Brazilian music *(é claro!).* This explains my affection for *feijoada* ((pronounced fey-joh-a-dah), which is a serious gastronomic dish but also a simple one: it's a big stew of black beans with many different succulent meats cooked inside and is served with white rice, *farofa* (toasted manioc flour), collard greens, and orange sections. We Brazilians are very casual people and like to serve our meals buffet style — and *feijoada* is no exception. It's certainly also a dish for special occasions and celebrations, and, what's more, it's a lot of fun to prepare!

Most Americans are unfamiliar with *feijoada*, but are surprised to find how much they like it once they try it. In a way, *feijoada* is the perfect food; it's healthy because beans are loaded with fiber and low in calories. It's good for the adaptable vegetarian because of the beans (and they can easily ladle just that on their plates). It works for dedicated carnivores because there is an orgy of meats to choose from; it also accommodates the adventurous eater who wants to try the most exotic cuts of meat.

The recipe is very flexible because you can choose whatever kinds of meat you want to cook. Pig's feet? Yes. Pig's ears? Go for it. Beef cheeks? Absolutely. In a traditional *feijoada* any piece of meat from any kind of animal that can release a bit of flavor is thrown into the pan (that's why I use pig's ears, though I do remove the ears just before serving). So let yourself go when it comes to the kinds of meat you'll be using. There is a world of meats to explore beyond steaks, ribs, and shoulders and this is the ideal dish to venture into the land of unfamiliar cuts. Your best bets for finding these are by going to a good butcher or visiting ethnic markets, including Brazilian ones, of course.

The most common kinds of meat used in a typical *feijoada* are pork, beef, *carne seca*, and *linguiça*. *Carne seca* (in Portuguese this is also referred to as *carne-de-sol* or *charqui*) is somewhat inaccurately called jerk beef in English. It is a slab of lean meat that is salt-cured and naturally sun-dried, resulting in a slightly chewy, textured meat with a deep red tone. While many of the ingredients found in the United States are comparable to those found in Brazil, this is not the case with *carne seca*; the American jerk beef is really a sweet-tangy, mildly salty snack sold in small packages of thin meat strips that have been rubbed or marinated and dehydrated, while the Brazilian version of *carne seca* needs to be reconstituted and de-salted before used in cooking.

You can also use *linguiça,* which is a Portuguese sausage widely used in Brazil that is made from cured pork meat flavored with onion, garlic, fat, and lots of spices. However, if you'd prefer to use Spanish *chorizo,* which is cured pork sausage spiced with paprika, it will be just as wonderful. We don't have *chorizo* in Brazil, but it's similar enough to *linguiça* to be the perfect substitute for it in the United States.

Feijoada showcases an overlooked skill more essential than any braising or sautéing: the skill of seasoning. Too salty, forget it. Not enough pepper equals boring. To my taste, the perfect *feijoada* has a dash of Worcestershire sauce, a generous pinch of salt, tons of onions and garlic, scallions, bell peppers, and Tabasco is a must. Most importantly, the beans must have a deep taste of meat.

Stewing techniques are also crucial; serve one hard piece of meat and your guests will think the worst of Brazilian food. The meats of a *feijoada* should be sliding off the bone — dark as ebony, succulent, and juicy. It doesn't really matter what kind of meats you use as long as you keep one rule in mind: If you use a lot of salted or greasy meats, you have to cook the meats in one batch of beans and make another one to serve, as the beans might get too fatty or too salty (especially when *carne seca* is used). If the dish is too salty, transfer the meats from the beans you cooked into the new beans and don't worry, the beans will still carry tons of meat flavor. In my own interpretation of *feijoada*, the meats are sautéed before adding them to the beans. I think searing meats in a hot pan coated with a thin film of oil producing a sizzling noise adds a great flavor to the crust of the meat (never crowd the pan and make sure to pat dry the meats before cooking).

If you are looking for fine dining, *feijoada* is not the dish for you. There is nothing fancy about it. It's almost as simple as rice and beans but that hasn't stopped a few restaurants from building a reputation around the dish. *Feijoada* is very generous to its associates; it gives rice and beans (our daily sustenance) a reason to party. It gives collard greens the dignity of a side dish, and oranges the noble role of a salad. Furthermore, *feijoada* is the kind of dish that hasn't suffered from urban overexposure, even in Brazil. In a way, I like it because it remains truthful to what the dish really is — as if you're eating a piece of history.

There are two theories concerning the origin of the dish. Some believe that it was created by the Brazilian slaves back in colonial times, using many leftovers from any animal, while others believe the dish was inspired by European stews with meats and sausages cooked in beans. The origin of *feijoada* means little to most modern Brazilians. What matters for many of us nowadays is that it has turned into a beloved tradition on Saturdays.

My obsession for *feijoada* has gradually increased over the years, though I must admit that when I first moved here I didn't prepare it as often as I do now and relied instead on rice and beans. As the years pass by and my soul seeks ever more "travel time" in the kitchen, the cooking of this dish brings me joy, evoking memories of myself as a healthy young woman, cycling at ease and peace on the boardwalks of Ipanema beach. It reminds me of a life well-lived in Rio.

In Brazil, *feijoada* casts a spell; it weakens and captivates the Brazilian spirit. A glass of caipirinha might get you ready to dance as you are slurping the last bite of meat while cleaning the sides of your mouth with black bean juices. *Feijoada* is the culinary equivalent of happiness, and whatever it is that you need to do afterwards, most likely it will end in samba.

FEIJOADA

(MEAT AND BLACK BEAN STEW) *Serves 8-10*

Serve feijoada with rice, farofa *(a traditional accompaniment made from manioc flour), collard greens, and orange and grapefruit salad.*

4 cups dried black beans, picked and rinsed

4 quarts cold water

4 tablespoons canola oil

4 pieces oxtail, about 1¼ pounds

1 pound top round, cut into big chunks

1 *linguiça* or *chorizo,* about 1 pound

½ pound pancetta, cut into medium-size cubes

½ cup chopped onions

½ cup chopped celery

½ cup chopped leeks (white part only)

½ cup chopped shallots

½ cup chopped scallions

2 tablespoons minced garlic

3 bay leaves

Kosher salt

Freshly ground black pepper

Ground nutmeg

Paprika

Cayenne pepper

Tabasco sauce

Worcestershire sauce

Place the beans in a very large pot and cover with the cold water. Bring to a boil over high heat. Turn heat to medium and cook, covered, for 1 hour, until the beans are just cooked, showing no traces of starch, but not mushy. The water will be dark but still clear. Remove from the heat and set aside. (You can cook the beans in a pressure cooker if you want to save time, and it will only take you 15 to 25 minutes.)

Meanwhile, start preparing the meats and vegetables. Pour enough of the oil in a large sauté pan over high heat to just thinly coat the bottom. Sear the oxtail, top round, and sausage in batches until browned on all sides. Transfer to a large bowl and cover tightly with aluminum foil to keep moist.

Heat the remaining oil in an extra-large Dutch oven pan, over medium heat, and cook the pancetta until lightly crispy. Add the onions, celery, leeks, shallots and scallions and cook, stirring occasionally, until tender, 3 to 5 minutes. Add the garlic and bay leaves, stir to blend. Add the beans and their liquid, and bring to a boil.

Cut the sausage into thirds and add it and the other meats and any accumulated juices from the bowl to the pan. Cover the pan and simmer over low heat for about 3 hours, until the meats are tender and falling off the bones. Season to taste with salt, pepper, nutmeg, paprika, cayenne, Tabasco, and Worcestershire.

From *The Brazilian Kitchen* by Leticia Moreinos Schwartz, © 2010. Used by permission from Kyle Books.

Bart Potenza and his partner, Joy Pierson, have founded three successful vegetarian dining establishments, including Candle Cafe (the first restaurant to be certified by the Green Restaurant Association) and Candle 79, one of the first upscale organic vegan restaurants in the United States. Bart is a leading proponent of health-food marketing and vegetarianism, and he has lectured and written widely on the virtues of healthy eating. He is the author of *Look Two Ways on a One-Way Street,* and he and Joy co-authored *The Candle Cafe Cookbook* (with Barbara Scott-Goodman). Bart is also a proud member of Co-op America, Social Venture Network, Business Leaders for Sensible Priorities, The Presidents Club at F.A.R.M., P.E.T.A., and Farm Sanctuary.

ALL'S WELL THAT EATS WELL

Bart Potenza

It all begins with boiling the water or maybe with the chopping of the vegetables. I'm very, very lucky because I've always enjoyed the tactile part of "creating a meal" — the movement in the kitchen, the sounds of the dishes, pots, and utensils in the preparation. The whole activity of stirring and tossing food always appealed to me. Fortunately, after cooking I find the cleaning and reorganization to be a Zen experience that grounds me and helps me to embrace my meal with loved ones and family, when all is complete.

With a background in marketing and art, little did I know that I would wind up in the restaurant business over twenty-six years ago. And why not?! My Italian-American heritage exposed me to a most magnificent rainbow of food.

In growing up I had eighteen aunts and uncles living in my Brooklyn community and each of their households presented a feast and an abundance of food on an ongoing basis. Those families ate and dined on every part of every animal because that's what they knew and believed in. I ate the same way, too!

Needless to say, those early days of food adventures had nothing to do with my eventual decision to become vegan. That happened to me when I was in my fifties. Now, in my seventeenth year of being a vegan and at age seventy-three, I continue to have more health and vitality than most thirty year olds.

However, those early experiences planted the seeds for my future destiny of being in the organic restaurant business. My sensual food legacy that was cultivated back then had to do with seasonings, sauces, gravies, and the extreme freshness of the ingredients that my relatives used. I've now taken that to a whole new level. At times I feel like Obi-Wan Kenobi when creating a meal. It's more of an intuitive experience that's totally enhanced by the abundance of green markets and local farms in the New York City area where I live. I can call myself a locavore for eight to ten months a year and this applies to my restaurants as well.

Another amazing ingredient for me is sharing this experience with my partner in life and in business, Joy Pierson. We journey to the farmers' markets in New York City and in

Connecticut, where we live on weekends. What a pleasure it is to share those moments with Joy, as we walk proudly with our recycled bags and green packaging and interact with ten to twelve farmers. After years of doing this, they know us well and more often than not they share their abundant seasonal crops so that they overflow our bags.

I enjoy being a minimalist when preparing a meal that involves a feast of ingredients — leeks, onions, shallots, garlic, ginger, and scallions. Stir-fry combos are my ultimate favorite, with a base of brown rice or soba noodles. Of course, I also love adding kale, bok choy, escarole, or tempeh (a fermented soy bean product high in protein) when preparing one of these recipes.

A lot of chopping, cleaning, and peeling happens next. The leeks, bok choy, and greens need a fair amount of rinsing, as the soil has embedded itself in the leaves and stems of these beauties.

The instrument of cutting and chopping that I love using is my Japanese Caddie knife. Favored by macrobiotic cooks, its flat, rectangular cutting surface and handle always feel comfortable with my grip and, at a cost of about forty dollars, it's certainly financially manageable for most home cooks.

Many of my friends and our restaurant chefs use a great

variety of knives. Most choices are dictated by the dish being prepared and the functions required for the incredible number of meals that call for slicing and dicing the rainbow of fruits and vegetables that we use. Chefs have been known to spend hundreds of dollars on a knife and their commitment to this cutting instrument can be very intense. Most of them travel home with their knives at the end of the day for fear that someone might use or tamper with their blade. I've noticed through the years that when we interview and train a new cook, they often arrive with their own cherished set of knives. For some reason, the young people arriving from the culinary schools have a full collection of cutting tools that they adore and use proudly. As an aside, we've not had much luck hiring men and women from the cooking schools. They may have great knives, but they usually have no clue about the intensity of working in or running a busy restaurant kitchen.

We bought a wonderful stainless steel sauté pan last year and it has been well-seasoned with a variety of oils and marinades to balance all the flavors we invite into its heavenly heat. Our repertoire of ingredients also includes a great organic olive oil, a bit of wheat-free tamari, and a touch of a hot sauce to spice it up a bit, and toasted sesame oil as well.

Let the games begin.

Stir-fry is practically a no-miss dish because the ingredients are so compatible that they hand off each other's flavors in a layered, intertwined way so that the finished product becomes a symphony of all the pieces. Once all the ingredients are assembled and placed in the pan, the cooking time — with lots of flipping and stirring of veggies — takes about twelve to fifteen minutes. I like covering the whole pan at that point so the veggies can continue to steam and sweat down so that all the flavors join together for a wonderful, finished recipe.

At times I cook up a separate, fast-cooking small pot of quinoa, one of my favorite grains, to round out the dish so that in the end I get not only a tasty meal, but a nutritious one as well. It's also quite wonderful to add a mesclun and baby green salad to the dining experience, along with some avocado and sliced fresh tomatoes. A nice vinaigrette will usually be our dressing of choice or a wonderful olive oil and balsamic vinegar would be another option.

Now, wait a minute, hold the presses, it's time to indulge in another piece of this scenario, the pouring of a vintage, full-bodied red wine. This brings me back to my childhood again.

From the age of twelve to seventeen years I used to help make homemade white and red wine with my Italian grandpa and my uncle. Oh, what a ritual! I don't even know why I took so much to helping him, but I looked forward to it every fall season. I even had a favorite plaid shirt that I would wear for the occasion. The pressing of the grapes and the storing of the previous year's vintage would happen in the basement of my grandpa's house.

A chute was set up each time to allow the cases of grapes to be delivered below to the basement, without undue strain on us or bruising of the grapes. The activity of pressing and straining the grapes took the better part of two weeks because everything had to be carefully measured and judged for taste and quality. Since this all happened over fifty years ago, in hindsight I mostly remember the smells, the teamwork, and of course the fabulous hand press that squeezed every bit of juice out of every bit of grape. The remains were a solid and somewhat juicy combo of squeezed grapes and stems and to my knowledge my grandpa and uncle composted them in a small garden that they used for growing vegetables.

Alas, the meal that I have now prepared will be joined by a glass or two of red wine. Yes, I say red! To this day the white wines don't generally satisfy me. I find them too light and mostly too sweet. However, when I drink a favorite full-bodied and rich-tasting red wine, my sense memory goes back to that cellar where I drank Grandpa's blend.

When it came to dining as a family, Grandpa used to sit at the head of the table. He was a jolly man who looked like Santa Claus, with a big belly and a handlebar mustache, and he liked to smoke a pipe. His name was Bartholomeo, as is mine, now shortened to Bart. I mostly remember the Sunday meals because they were multi-family and ended with delicious desserts such as cannoli, zeppole, fresh baked pies, and usually a large fruit bowl with mixed nuts. Of course, the espresso coffee that followed added another nuance to the card playing that rolled out after each meal. What fun!

Now I sit at the head of the table at home and at both Candle Cafe and Candle 79, where loved ones now indulge in the vegan versions of the same desserts.

Thank you, Grandpa, for giving me my name and planting the seeds for the joy of food and wine in my life. *Buon appetito!*

∞ ∞ ∞

The stir-fry I describe in my essay was inspired by a number of dishes, including the Ginger-Miso Stir-fry recipe (next page) that appears in *The Candle Cafe Cookbook*. Of course, I added my own special touches to the version in the essay and I invite you to do the same whenever possible.

GINGER-MISO STIR-FRY

Serves 4-6

Stir-fries are so versatile and fun to make. We like to use the freshest vegetables we can find from local farmers' and Asian markets. Feel free to improvise your own stir-fry, adding your favorite vegetables with this quick and easy recipe. It's great when served over brown rice or soba noodles.

GINGER-MISO SAUCE

1 cup water

1 tablespoon minced garlic

¼ cup minced fresh ginger

½ cup mellow white miso

¼ cup agave nectar

¼ cup shoyu

2 tablespoons toasted sesame oil

Pinch crushed red pepper flakes

STIR-FRY

3 tablespoons olive oil

1½ teaspoons minced garlic

1½ teaspoons minced fresh ginger

½ cup seeded, deveined, and sliced red bell peppers

½ cup seeded, deveined, and sliced yellow peppers

¾ cup sliced onions

½ cup sliced and blanched bok choy

½ cup cut and blanched string beans

1½ cups cut and blanched broccoli

1 cup chopped shredded cabbage

½ cup stemmed and sliced shiitake mushrooms

1 cup cubed tofu, rinsed and drained

¼ cup thinly sliced water chestnuts

¼ cup sesame seeds

To make the Ginger-Miso Sauce, place all of the ingredients in a blender and blend until smooth. The sauce will keep in the refrigerator, covered, for up to a week.

For the stir-fry, heat the olive oil in a large sauté pan or wok over high heat. Add the garlic and ginger and sauté for about 2 minutes.

Add the vegetables and tofu and toss to combine. Continue to sauté and toss the vegetables and tofu together until you reach the desired doneness, 5 to 10 minutes, depending on your taste.

Add the Ginger-Miso Sauce and water chestnuts and stir-fry for an additional 3 minutes. Sprinkle with sesame seeds and serve at once.

This recipe is reprinted from *The Candle Cafe Cookbook* by Joy Pierson and Bart Potenza with Barbara Scott-Goodman (Clarkson Potter). Used by permission of Clarkson Potter/Publishers, an imprint of the Crown Publishing Group, a division of Random House, Inc.

Mika Takeuchi is a Tokyo-born, California-based writer and entrepreneur who founded the Web site/blog, FoodFashionista. com — dedicated to her passion for all things culinary. Mika's love of gastronomy and travel began as a child; since then, she has ventured across the globe, dining and seeking out dishes from street food to haute cuisine. She was a guest explorer/writer for the *Michelin Guide* and an ambassador for Luce Wines. Mika and her companies have been featured in the *Washington Post, Lucky, San Francisco Magazine, 7x7* magazine, and many more.

FEEDING THE SOUL
AND THE SENSES

Mika Takeuchi

Being aligned with Mother Nature makes my soul feel alive, whether hiking unpaved dirt paths in the Hawaiian rainforests or swimming in the crystal clear, aqua-blue waters of the Caribbean surrounded by sea turtles. When I am in close proximity to my environment — on land or in the sea — I feel nourished from the inside out. In fact, I believe that the way the earth nourishes us is Mother Nature's greatest gift to us all.

I've tasted food all around the globe, from three-star Michelins in Europe to the break-of-dawn sushi counters at the Tsukiji Fish Market in Tokyo to ripened, organic Japanese persimmons from my uncle's backyard in California. Although each of these three experiences varied considerably, they are all linked by a common thread: the use of fresh, high-quality ingredients. There is something so invigorating and satisfying about enjoying a meal straight from the source, with food that is seasonal and locally grown in the region where you are living or visiting.

On a magical, unforgettable trip to Umbria, Italy, I felt a strong connection to the surrounding land and all that was cultivated on it. Not only did I gain a full understanding and knowledge of what it was like to live off the land, but I learned what it was like to live *abundantly* off the land. At a dear friend's twelfth-century villa, Torre Olivola in the medieval town of Todi, I was surrounded for miles in all directions by landscapes you would only see in the most picturesque paintings.

Lush, well-tended gardens of fresh fruits and vegetables, just steps from the historic countryside villa, were lit up with the vibrant colors of the tomatoes, radicchio, eggplants, bell peppers, and blood oranges. In every area of this vast, serene, tranquil paradise were perfectly placed benches or sets of tables and chairs where one could sip morning tea or cappuccino while basking in the glory of it all. It was a heavenly way to start the day, with the toasty sun rays shining down upon you, the sound of chirping birds, the rustling foliage, and the breath of the crisp, unpolluted wind whispering sweet nothings and reminding me this was all real, not a dream.

A five-minute walk led me to a honeybee colony where these hard-working, vitally necessary, tiny buzzing critters would labor all day, 24/7, creating their sweet pollinated gifts from the floral nectars. This magnificent honey, golden in color with a creamy yet thick and silky smooth consistency, was delectable on the artisanal walnut bread produced by the local Italian baker, or drizzled over yogurt and fresh bright peaches, plums, and strawberries in the morning. I felt true appreciation towards the worker bees for all their generous hard work. With one drop of magnificent zest from the luxurious honey, you could tell they put their heart and soul into their sweet creation.

In Italy, they love to eat. The whole visit, I knew I was in the right place. Slow food, real food, good food — that is what our days consisted of from morning to night. Even though we were eating three- to five-course meals for lunch and dinner daily, I never felt overly stuffed or uncomfortable, and I never regretted eating anything — none of this wonderfully tantalizing food was "bad" for me.

In addition to mealtimes, the Europeans have this lovely thing called siesta, which in my opinion is a politically correct term that other nations should freely adopt. If more people had it, there would be a greater sense of enjoyment to one's day and life. Siesta is a time for rest after a midday meal. It allows you to have enough time to come home during your workday and enjoy a real meal, instead of being rushed, stuffing your face as you stand looking at the clock ticking away the last dreaded second of your sixty-minute lunch break. It allows you to have time to prepare a quality meal and to spend that time with the people you love, so that when you go back to work later in the afternoon, you feel rejuvenated, satisfied, and ready to get back to your duties.

Torre Olivola was surrounded by leafy, branched olive trees that provided shade from the sunlight that stretched across Umbria to the Tuscan border. More importantly, these olive trees produced the most succulent olives that were hand-picked and later cold-pressed, yielding the finest-quality extra-virgin olive oil in varying rich green hues. We savored the olive oil with a number of accompaniments, such as fresh crusty Italian bread, tomato and garlic bruschetta, and pasta (*al dente,* of course). We also brushed it over fresh local seafood and vegetables, like sautéed mushrooms, grilled eggplant, and blanched green beans. The tasty, fruity aromas of succulent, high-quality olive oil are not its only reward; the health and beauty benefits attributed to olive oil, with its polyphenols and antioxidants, are a welcome added bonus of this Italian staple as well.

As far as the eye could see, and from a glance out of almost every window at Torre Olivola, were breathtaking views of stretches of vineyard. Grapes are known as "the fruit of the gods" and in Italy, wine is not only enjoyed, it is worshipped. At this ancient fortress where I was staying, the vineyard grapes were delicately hand-picked, produced, bottled, and aged at just the right altitude in the finest oak barrels. These barrels were stored in the villa's remarkable underground cantina, creating the most magnificent 100 percent merlot. Along with the villa's main dining room, it was here in the cantina with the wood-burning stove and the hanging, curing *cinta senese* (Italian black pig) that we clinked each other's wine glasses over the most incredible rustic home-cooking. The meals were also a rich visual feast with tables adorned with colorful Grazia majolica ceramic dishes from nearby Deruta, and organic centerpieces created from the gardens' harvest.

About a mile away was the property's farm of free-range black pigs that produce the most superior charcuterie. These free-range pigs are acorn-fed and are considered the most elite of the swine. Even the top local restaurants purchased the meat from the villa's farm. Nearby farms supplied parmigiano-reggiano, pecorino, provolone, taleggio, and sheep's milk cheese along with hand-crafted, preservative-free butter. My favorite cheese, burrata, which is a creamy mozzarella, was picked up at an unassuming, yet wondrous spot just off the highway on the way to Todi. Cheese was a part of every meal: shaved parmesan over vegetable soup; warm taleggio, provolone, and sliced pear crostini; and the classic caprese salad with tomatoes, basil, and mozzarella.

Of the four seasons in Italy, there isn't one that doesn't hold some allure for me, but a particularly cherished time of year is "truffle season" — months when the underground growing fungi reach maturity, and are ready to be discovered by well-trained dogs or sniffing hogs. These *tartufi* (as the Italians call them) come in several forms, including the more prevalent black, and the rare, highly sought-after, and pricey white form. Umbrian black truffles are usually hunted from November to March, while white truffles are usually found from October to December. I absolutely delight in the fragrant white truffles and always feel so blessed when I can consume them in any way, over tagliatelle or atop scrambled eggs. With a touch of white truffle, I never want or need any other spice to conflict with the pure aphrodisiacal taste. It's like superior-quality raw fish; you don't want to mask or drown the flawless essence of flavor with soy sauce. Truffles are a true gift from the earth, definitely one of the highest on the food chain as far as I'm concerned.

Besides the astounding natural company I was surrounded by — honeybees, olive trees, grapevines, black pigs, fungi growing underground, and a multitude of vegetative growth — the time spent at Torre Olivola was made even more ideal by the authentic, loving, fellow gourmands who shared this edible organic splendor with me. They were inspirational people who had lived fully and well, and I aspired to be like them. We delighted each day in fascinating conversation that ranged over such topics as art, music, travel, politics, and the list goes on. Not only was my stomach well-sustained, but my mind was actively feasting during our daily meals together. From hearty farro soup, to warm radicchio salad with parmesan slices and balsamic vinegar, to the vibrant seven-item tuna salad that resembled a garden party, I held dear to the fact that great company makes great food taste even better. This was and will always be a treasured time with awe-inspiring friends over excellent meals and wine.

So what did I bring back home from this experience that can be applied to everyday life? While eating sustainable, unprocessed food has always been my priority, my time in Torre Olivola reminded me that simple is often superior. The key to optimal cooking starts with quality ingredients. Never underestimate the value of mealtime and treasured time spent with loved ones. I understand that not everyone can dine in a twelfth-century castle with a neighboring farm of black pigs and vineyards; that's not my daily reality either. But I constantly aim to make conscious choices about the food I am purchasing and putting into my body since that is my castle. No matter where one lives, you can establish a habit of supporting your local farmers, and even growing your own produce. Eating fresh, healthy, and well-balanced meals is easier than you think and it truly does feed the soul and the senses.

PEAR AND CHEESE CROSTINI   *Serves 4*

1 thin loaf baguette bread (can use whole wheat
   for healthier option), sliced ⅓ inch thick

3 tablespoons extra-virgin olive oil

4 ounces provolone or taleggio cheese (you can also combine
   both for varied taste), cut into slices

2 pears (organic recommended), very thinly sliced

3 teaspoons honey (raw, unadulterated recommended)

Prepare an aluminum foil-covered skillet over medium-high heat.

Place the bread slices in a single layer in the skillet and brush with the olive oil. After 30 seconds, turn over and brush the other side with olive oil for 30 seconds. Repeat.

Remove the skillet from the heat and place the cheese slices over the bread. If using both cheeses, you can combine the slices of both. Top with the pear slices.

Return the skillet to medium-high heat and, once the cheese starts to melt, wait 15 seconds and remove from the heat.

Drizzle the honey on top of the crostini. Serve immediately.

Ronald Holden is a Seattle-based journalist with over twenty years of experience in both print and broadcast media. For fifteen years he also operated a luxury travel company, France In Your Glass. His online journal about food, wine, and travel, Cornichon. org, was named one of the "Ten Best Food Blogs on the Internet" by About.com.

LASAGNA YOU'LL LOVE

Ronald Holden

I once had a foie gras *raviolo* at the George V in Paris, a cube of unctuous goose liver inside a plump pillow of pasta. One bite for 35 euros, an epiphany: a transcendent mouthful of pleasure.

That memorable, if costly, experience sent me on a quest for more of the same, so, lately, I've been writing a series of articles for Crosscut.com (often cross-posted on my own blog, Cornichon.org) that profile a restaurant in Seattle, through the lens of a single, signature dish. Pieces about a crab cake, a Wagyu steak, a chicken liver mousse, a Dutch baby pancake, even a locally brewed beer. Delicious all, each in its own way.

But I have a personal favorite, the lasagna bolognese at a modest Italian place on Queen Anne, Enza Cucina Siciliana.

Allow me a bit of explanation, using local examples.

Restaurants come in three basic body types, if you haven't already figured it out. Not categorical, and variations exist, of course. And we're not talking about "theme" restaurants that serve nothing but burgers or pizza.

First, there's Corporate. Owned and operated by (not necessarily competent) hospitality industry "experts," with multiple establishments run by (not necessarily competent) hired hands. From the number of sunflower seeds atop a salad to the size of the waiter's bow tie, it's in the book. They can be admirable (Consolidated Restaurants, for example, owns both Elliott's Oyster House and Metropolitan Grill) but they're run by the book and by the numbers (and Consolidated dumped Union Square Grill when the numbers no longer added up).

Second, the so-called chef-driven restaurants, staffed by pros with (at least some) formal culinary training. These are the places that get the press, the reviews, the traffic. This is where the James Beard winners practice their craft: Ethan Stowell, Jason Wilson, William Belickis, Kevin Davis, and Maria Hines. They often have angel financing (so they can afford new equipment and a full staff), though deep pockets can be a mixed blessing: Just ask Justin Niedermeyer or Dan Thiessen, bounced from Cascina Spinasse and 0/8 Seafood Grill respectively when their backers became disenchanted.

Third, the family kitchen, where Mamma's behind the stove, Dad's at the door or tending bar, and Sis or Sonny waits tables. These places, located along every neighborhood's main drag, can be wildly inconsistent, not so much for the food (though their menus can try too hard to please everyone) but for the rest of the dining experience, ambiance, and service.

Which brings us to Enza's, where a clientele of adventurous diners dig into a rotating selection of home-cooked Sicilian specialties and her particularly popular lasagna bolognese.

By now, I have become great friends with Enza and her extended restaurant-owning family (Mondello, La Mondellina, La Vita e Vita è Bella). They're not quite sure what to make of me, since my German-Jewish background is virtually the opposite of Sicilian (though similar in its clannishness and emphasis on family). I think of myself as their *consigliere*: I noodle around with their Web sites, menus, and newsletters, and help Enza (who speaks very little English) with cross-cultural translations.

So, call my love for the lasagna suspect, but once you try it, you'll agree with me.

გა გა გა

Enza herself makes every lasagna herself, by hand, either in half-pans (for takeout) or full hotel pans. A tiny woman in her sixties, full of energy, she becomes a one-person assembly line as she dips the pasta into boiling water, spoons and smooths the fillings, tosses handfuls of cheese into each layer. She does this in a commissary kitchen in Magnolia, two miles from her own place atop Queen Anne, a kitchen she inhabits six mornings a week to cook and bake the staples for all her family's restaurants. Watching her work, one observer, who'd spent decades in the galleys of merchant ships, called her a mechanic, his highest praise.

The pasta starts with Morbread Unbleached Flour and Number One Semolina, both from Pendleton Mills and delivered in fifty-pound bags. It's mixed with eggs, water, and salt in proportions Enza knows and adjusts as required by weather conditions, then rolled into sheets by an Italian-made Emiliomiti pasta machine. The bolognese sauce is made with canned San Marzano tomatoes imported from Italy and locally sourced beef, long-simmered in five-gallon batches until the meat virtually dissolves into the sauce.

The secret ingredient is the addition of a deceptively simple bechamel sauce that's spooned into each of the lasagna's eight layers. Bechamel, if you've misplaced your kitchen glossary, is the basic white sauce: butter, flour, milk, salt, touch of nutmeg. Enza makes at least one batch a day in her favorite kitchen appliance, a Swiss-made contraption called Thermomix that's part Cuisinart, part double-boiler. Pile in the ingredients, set the timer to sixteen minutes, and it makes a smooth, luscious sauce. Once the lasagna is assembled, the hotel pan goes into the oven to set; individual servings are cut and heated to order.

The result is nothing short of ethereal. Most of the lasagnas I've eaten over the years have tasted like wet cardboard separated by layers of cheese goo. Enza's lasagna is substantial but not heavy, richly flavorful but not over the top with non-traditional non-essentials. Sure, there are folks who make lasagna with elk, oysters, offal. Not saying they're not tasty, but they're not lasagna bolognese, an Italian comfort food as basic as meatloaf.

∽ ∽ ∽

The lasagna has found a legion of admirers, including other restaurants. It's the only non-pizza item on the menu at the Via Tribunali chain.

One gent who ordered it at the Tribunali on Capitol Hill was so taken by it that he made his way across town and was amazed to encounter Mamma Enza, whom he had met years ago when she was cooking at La Vita è Bella in Belltown. Big hugs all around. That amazing lasagna, could he get a double order to go? Sure can. As it happens, I was behind the bar that afternoon, so I poured the man a Prosecco and we chatted about the the clan's various restaurants (after Belltown, opening Mondello in Magnolia, Divino Wine Bar on Ballard Avenue, then her own place), while Enza packed up his order. (Instructions for the lasagna? Fifteen minutes in a 350°F oven.) He took a copy of the menu (the lasagna's $15 at dinner) and handed me his card, which I swiped through the Dinerware computer: SCHULTZ/HOWARD.

Forty million customers walk into a Starbucks every week; that's a lot of coffee. The Starbucks CEO walking into Enza's, that we can handle. We didn't have to shut down for retraining or to reformulate the Frappuccino, either. But Howard, just don't expect free refills.

ᔕ ᔕ ᔕ

Vincisgrassi sounds like the title of an aria by Verdi or Bellini, doesn't it? (Imagine an evil basso singing *"Nessun mangia!"*) But, hey, it's just noodles. And noodles can be very tasty, as we know. Still, these are special.

Some background. Alfred, Prince of Windischgrätz, had a distinguished career as a general in the Austro-Hungarian army. At the end of the eighteenth century, he commanded the Marche region, south of the Po delta on Italy's eastern seaboard, where a local chef created a multi-layered pasta dish in his honor, a variant on a local dish called *prinzgrassi*. The original recipes called for various organ meats; today it's made with chicken livers or veal ragù. Over the years, tomatoes have found their way into the recipe alongside the bechamel sauce, and the spelling has evolved to *vincisgrassi*.

It's the Northern Italian flip-side of *lasagna al forno,* cartoon cat Garfield's red-sauce, oven-baked favorite. (Remember those giant bricks of frozen lasagna at Costco? It was a $50 million a year business for Michael Angelo's Gourmet Foods until Costco started making its own about a year ago.)

Now, before you start sending in comments about your favorite recipe, remember that the word lasagna actually refers to the ceramic dish used for cooking, like pot-au-feu or eintopf or, gee, "casserole."

One thing's for sure: a true *vincisgrassi* wouldn't use a "foreign" cheese like mozzarella, which comes from Naples. (Naples was literally a foreign country until Italian unification in 1861.) Ricotta, yes, that's as universal as cottage cheese. But in the north, cooks might also use a mild cow's milk cheese called stracchino, often melted atop pizzas. Even better, a "plastic" curd cheese called scamorza; like mozzarella, it's aged for a few days in the whey, then stretched and kneaded before molding. Smoked scamorza is even more flavorful and makes a lively complement to the traditional ingredients. Having developed the "hearty" *vincisgrassi* for La Vita è Bella, Enza Sorrentino uses pecorino and parmigiano for her milder version at her own place on Queen Anne.

ের ের ের

There are days, I know, that Enza wishes she'd never have to make another lasagna in her life. Like any artist, she wants to create new things, and she feels held back by all those tickets asking for yet another order. Was this how Vivaldi felt, why Vivaldi kept composing the same concerto, with but minor variations, over and over? Bach wrote magnificently original music every week as the archbishop's Kappellmeister and never complained. Enza knows that she'll have to hire kitchen workers to make the lasagna, eventually. For now, she's still behind the stove every morning, as elegantly dressed as a Milan fashion model, doggedly defending the flavors of *l'antica cucina rustica,* Italy's historic culture of country cooking. A culinary tradition well worth preserving and savoring, down to the last bite.

Louisa Chu is a chef and food journalist. She graduated from Le Cordon Bleu Paris, staged at el Bulli and Alinea, and worked as a chef in Alaska. Her work has appeared in *Gourmet, CHOW,* the *Chicago Tribune,* and the *Chicago Sun-Times.* She has also appeared on the television shows *Iron Chef America* (as a judge), *No Reservations,* and *Gourmet's Diary of a Foodie.*

CRÊPE COMPLÈTE

Louisa Chu

The boom echoed so loud it sounded like the truck had T-boned another. I couldn't imagine that she'd survived. I actually saw her roll over — end over end — or was it side over side? It was, as these moments are, a slow-motion blur. But she landed back on her feet, her eyes fixed, head gyroscoping around, still chasing the cat, never losing sight of it. The truck that had hit her was a small, white box on wheels. Thank God for the petite delivery trucks of France. Before we knew it, half the town was on the street surrounding us. The busboy at our *crêperie* ran out so fast that he was still up to his elbows in dish soap bubbles. Before I saw Karli get back up, I thought, "How am I going to bring my dead dog back to the U.S.?" I could not believe she was alive. But then I thought, maybe she's still in shock. You read about it all the time, beings that don't know they should be dead, who survive for a few minutes on adrenaline alone, before they realize the severity of the situation, and then expire. When I finally got to her, her short lifetime with us had flashed before my eyes. I held her tight and close in relief. She was shaking. Or maybe I was shaking. Luckily, there was no blood — no bones jutting out at odd angles. She seemed to be intact. If anything she was still trembling from the excitement of having chased a wily French village cat.

If she met her end in France it would have been fitting because Karli became ours in part because of Champagne and caviar. I should explain. My boyfriend at the time and I had decided that the next step we should take in our relationship would be to get a dog. Two dogs actually. Specifically, a pair of German Shepherd puppies from a breeder who bred dogs from the original Rin Tin Tin line. On their Web site I ogled the different colors of dogs. The classic tri-color? All black? Blond?

And then, one morning, driving to see my therapist — before I go further, I should explain again: We were living in Beverly Hills at the time. In an apartment, not a mansion, in the so-called flatlands below the hills, though I did run into locals like Jack Nicholson at Pavilions grocery store and Keifer Sutherland at the bar at the Avalon Hotel (on the night I saw him he jumped into the pool fully clothed). So you see it was almost a requirement to have a therapist. Change your address with the DMV, get a therapist — not necessarily in that order. So that morning, driving to my therapist, I saw a vision of a dog. She was blonde, German Shepherd-shaped, and walked with a determination that made me pull over to ask her owner about what kind of breed her dog was. Her owner said she thought she was a Lab-Shepherd mix and within minutes the woman tried to give her to me. What had this dog done that she was on the chopping block? The dog was anxious to get going, but good-naturedly so.

I didn't know then that the dog — named Carly (after Carly Simon) and whose cat brother was named Lionel (as in Ritchie) — apparently was never walked. In fact, she'd hardly ever been out of her Beverly Hills backyard during her entire four years of life. And worse, she had a big picture window to watch the world pass her by. Some dog lover in the neighborhood, we'd learn later, had actually paintballed the house, posting a note that read, "You don't deserve this dog!"

I didn't know any of that then. The first time I saw Carly I didn't know she would become my dog, my first dog. I thanked the woman for the offer of her dog, on the spot, on the side of the street, and said maybe I could just walk the dog sometime.

I almost forgot about Carly — tried to anyway — until the night after the caviar and Champagne tasting at the Wine House on the west side of Los Angeles.

Sadly it doesn't take much for me to get drunk. So after what couldn't have been more than sips that totaled a single flute I was blotto. My sister drove home, past Carly's window. We'd seen her on the way, too. We then saw her in the window just about every time we drove down Charleville — pronounced Charlie Ville by the locals. Day and night — on our way to and from jobs, errands, events — there she was.

Emboldened by the Champagne, I decided to go get Carly for a walk. Her owner didn't seem surprised when we called or showed up at her door to take her dog. She seemed more happy to see visitors — someone who wasn't her ex or there for her sullen teens and pre-teen — than aware of the fact that someone was there to walk her dog. *My dog* — from that first walk she was my dog. Shortly thereafter, before the official handover months later, I changed the spelling of her name. She didn't mind.

After that caviar-and-Champagne-fueled first walk, after making a failed bid to buy a beautiful, mid-century modern gem of a house in the hills overlooking Eagle Rock, we decided — just four months later — to treat ourselves to a trip to the south of France as our consolation prize for losing the house.

And that's how we ended up on the street corner just outside the stone wall that surrounded the old city in Saint-Rémy de

Provence, Karli just having been hit by a small white French delivery truck.

We'd started the vacation landing in Nice at night, where the waiters at Le Safari on le Cours Saleya knelt down, all the better to rub Karli behind the ears, while chic Côte d'Azur tourists desperately tried to order something to eat or drink. We, on the other hand, were plied with baskets full of crisp-crusted and satisfyingly chewy baguettes with briny tapenade and sautéed baby octopus, about the size (and just as tender) as a baby's fist. The rosé never stopped flowing while our dog-less *terrasse-mates* waved in futile attempts to flag down a waiter.

We only stayed a couple of nights, but each evening, as dinnertime rolled around, we selected a restaurant based on the most festively dressed tables set up each evening outside. We ate and drank while Karli, who'd only been ours a few weeks, ran wild in the streets of le Vieille Ville with other local dogs. She'd run off, play in some medieval church courtyard, run back for a bite of bread, or a swipe of coarse pâté, and then, fortified, dash off again. She always came back.

In Saint-Rémy our home base was L'Hôtel les Ateliers de l'Image, the village's old theater turned boutique hotel and photography gallery. From there we made daily excursions to Le Petit Duc, Anne Daguin's legendary cookie shop with sweets made from historic and ancient recipes. Would we taste a lavender sweet or rosemary savory? The stories behind each were almost better.

We stayed long enough so that we ran into regulars while walking, exchanging enough news, enquiring and responding *ça va's* to satisfy all parties involved.

Our hotel had a decent restaurant, where we had a pot-au-feu that warmed us enough to brave the first hints of *le mistral* — the infamous, madness-inducing, wild, and wicked wind — it was October after all. But it was La Farandole, the neighborhood crêperie on the corner where we found ourselves most often. Simple buckwheat *crêpes complète* — with salty ham, melted Gruyère, and runny-yolk egg — and dessert *crêpes* brimming with Nutella. Clichéd, not even regionally correct, but just what we all wanted.

It was from their kitchen that our soapy-armed busboy had run. We'd just exited the long, gravel driveway from the hotel grounds. Karli sighted the cat before we did. She dashed across the two-lane road that circled around the old-walled village center. The truck hit her square on her side, I now remember. I flew by her side in an instant and it seemed the entire village had, too. Short, black-clad, older Provençal ladies appeared faster than should have been possible. So did men who must have abandoned a dusty game of *pétanque*. Immediately, someone called the town vet just outside the village and told her to expect us. Offers poured in to drive us or at least escort us. Somehow we knew where the vet was, so off we sped. There had to be internal bleeding, I feared.

We pulled up at the same time as the vet. She did not speak English and somehow I suddenly understood veterinary French. She warned us of possible hemorrhaging. Yet she couldn't find anything, not even with the X-rays. Surely Karli would be *noir et bleu* and sore the next day she said.

But she was fine. Never a scratch. Never a bruise. Never slowed down.

Shortly after we returned to our calm terra cotta-tiled room, there was a soft knock at our door. The owner of the *crêperie* was there with our busboy, their arms laden with plates of what she already knew were our favorites. The room's somber mood was overwhelmed by the aroma of nutty, browned butter. She'd brought us dinner on real plates, to eat with real silverware. Chilled rosé with real glasses. And even a *crêpe complète* of her very own for Karli. Just what we all needed.

Karli ate. We ate. We drank. She slept.

The next day, she was fine. Not a scratch. Not a bruise. Never slowed down.

Anna Thomas wrote her first cookbook while she was a graduate student in film studies at UCLA. *The Vegetarian Epicure,* published in 1973, became a phenomenal success and remains a classic, widely acknowledged as the book that brought pleasure to vegetarian cuisine. *The Vegetarian Epicure, Book Two* followed in 1978, and *The New Vegetarian Epicure,* a menu-based cookbook, in 1996. Her latest book, *Love Soup,* recently won the James Beard Foundation Book Award in the Healthy Focus catergory. Anna Thomas is also known as a screenwriter and producer. Her principal credits include *El Norte,* for which she was nominated for an Academy Award, *A Time of Destiny, Frida,* and *My Family, Mi Familia.*

WHO IS AT THE TABLE?

Anna Thomas

What a lovely thing it is to plan a meal — whether it's done as a work of art or the comforting daily ritual of caring for the family — and I am daily grateful to be in that part of the world's population that enjoys this privilege: *to be able to plan a meal.* It is a gift to know that I will eat a meal when I expect to, that I might elevate it to an aesthetic experience, or just have a load of fun with it.

Damn lucky.

For several years I devoted a lot of time to planning meals. I was writing *The New Vegetarian Epicure,* which I had decided to structure entirely around menus — everything from extravagant parties to simple one-bowl meals. I enjoyed my pursuit of the perfect meal. Each one was like a little story, unfolding around my table. And as with any story, I found that the most important thing was the cast of characters. Who was at the table?

Some stories were family comedies, tales of nutrition and schedules and picky eaters. Some were fantasies, food as theater. And some were memories . . .

In a golden time, my husband and I and our new baby lived in the south of France, back when there were francs and there were ten of them to the dollar. We had just finished working like ants for several years to make a difficult film, and then had a baby in the last stages of that work. We were tired. Now, amazed at our powerful currency, we roamed the sun-washed countryside of Provence, visiting those exquisite restaurants that one finds only in the villages and country towns, the ones that are destinations. Each of those magical meals followed a ritual deeply rooted in the culture of that beautiful land.

In the summer, the dining rooms of these inns are unused. We arrived to find tables set out on a spacious terrace, looking out to a medieval village or a lavender field. Our reserved table was ours for the evening, because no one could be in a hurry here. An aperitif was brought — Champagne with cassis, or a local, herb-scented liqueur, and with it the *amuse-bouche*, a morsel of flaky pastry with something savory tucked inside, or a small plate of glistening, oily black olives. This was the détente, our landlord Jacques once explained to us, between the day and everything it contained . . . and the evening meal.

Now food and wine were discussed. In consultation with the pleasant maitre d', a menu was decided. The first course might be a green sorrel soup, tart and silky on the tongue, or it might be an unforgettable ratatouille, eggplants and onions and tomatoes ripened in the hot sun of a Provençal summer and cooked slowly in fruity olive oil. Or aioli, a breathtaking stab of raw garlic wrapped in a fresh mayonnaise. And a large purple-tipped artichoke to pull apart and dip into the sauce . . .

Then the drama of *loup de mer en papillote,* the delicate fillet of fish wrapped up like a gift in parchment, puffed and crisp from the heat of the oven. Sliced open, the fragrant steam escaped and enveloped me. Slivers of vegetables, aromatic herbs, wine . . . a world of flavor released just for me . . .

Salad, a few tender leaves, the vinaigrette gleaming in the fading light of the long summer evening. A platter of goat cheese, selected from dozens. We didn't pretend to know what we were doing, but we couldn't go wrong . . .

After the long conversations, the wine, the contemplative silence when a new course appeared and attention was given to tasting, we found ourselves under a dome of stars, and in front of us was a trolley laden with sweets. Chocolate mousse so dark it was almost black, bright red berries, fruit tarts . . . The largest plate of the meal was produced, and the waiter smiled. I chose white peach tart, thin slices of fruit layered over crème anglaise on a buttery crust. The waiter asked, "What else?" Now I understood. When we said yes to dessert, it meant all the desserts, whatever we wanted — yes, let's try them all, why not! Later still, there was a little *digestif,* a glass of *eau de vie* that seared my throat and spread through my body like another noonday sun, while the night air cooled my skin. What a good thing we'd booked a room in the village for the night.

Years went by. Back home in my California kitchen, working on *The New Vegetarian Epicure,* I remembered those long, languorous evenings when we were learning about food, learning to be a family, and feeling like the luckiest devils in the world. How could I devise a meal that would recall that feeling?

I didn't try to duplicate sophisticated restaurant food, because *I am not a restaurant!* And anyway, that wasn't the point. The point was — how to evoke the lavender in the air during the harvest, the sun at midday, the fragrance of wild thyme under our feet? The vivid colors and flavors, the interplay of rustic and refined, the sense of well-being . . .

My relaxed summer dinner party began with a salty and pungent tapenade of inky oil-cured olives, citrus zest, thyme, and rosemary. I served it with homemade crostini, toasted until their edges were brown and crunchy. And because I had garden tomatoes, red and dripping with juice, I added this quick salad. Chop chop — tomatoes, garlic, torn basil leaves, all bathed in oil and a sprinkle of sea salt. The first course was ready. Champagne was chilling for the aperitifs.

Next, a cold melon soup with mint cream. The sweetness of a perfectly ripe melon, tempered with white wine and lemon, and fresh mint leaves finely chopped into the cream — heaven. It brought back to me the Saturday market in Apt, the melon field across the road from our house.

I am a vegetarian cook, so I made a zucchini blossom risotto for the next course. The yellow flowers, shallots, and green squash were quickly sautéed, I simmered the rice until it was barely tender, then stirred in a rich finish of Parmesan cheese. The flecks of green and gold in the risotto were beautiful. (This was the only dish that needed to be made at the last moment, and I knew by then everyone would be ready for a break, ready to sip wine and keep me company while I stirred.)

For dessert, I chose something that could not be improved with any amount of work — ripe blackberries. I served them with crème anglaise made earlier that day and put away to chill. Tiny biscotti were passed with the coffee.

It was a meal for a soft summer night and a chilled glass of dry, crisp rosé. Remembering the relaxed Provençal terrace, I had set the table outside, draped it with a white cloth, and put a jug of wildflowers in the center. When I wrote up the menu notes for the book, I added, "Best eaten in a garden, with a slight sunburn on your shoulders . . ."

But the most important thing — who was at that table in the garden? My wonderful friends, the ones who love to argue about the wine and forget the argument after the first sip, who love to laugh and tell stories, who will stay up late, listening to the evening birds.

In that big, rambling house there were many dinner parties, and many family meals in the kitchen. Quesadillas pan-grilled in minutes, and roulades made with painstaking care.

Dinners for romance, for friendship, for celebration, and for sustenance. Many became the menus I described in my book. Then the kids grew up and went away, and I moved to a smaller house. While the new house was being renovated. I moved into an even smaller space, a converted painter's studio on the property — one room! I cleaned it up and tucked a tiny, temporary kitchen under the stairs to the sleeping loft. It was 81 inches wall-to-wall. All my kitchen equipment, my dishes, my *stuff* was in deep storage.

This was the big downsize. I thought it would kill me, until I realized I loved it.

I had assumed I wouldn't have another dinner party until I moved into the new house. But a few weeks in, I took my one cutting board and my one good knife, and pulled out the one big pot that wasn't packed away. I reached for the good olive oil, and started chopping an onion. Before long, a gorgeous white bean and pumpkin soup was simmering on the teensy stove. I sent out an email to my friends: "The soup kitchen is open."

One friend arrived with homemade bread, another with a big wedge of pecorino, and still another with a batch of roasted beets and some heirloom tomatoes which he began to slice into a salad. Someone had olives, someone had fava bean hummus, and chocolate appeared by magic. Wine was opened, glasses were raised.

I had not told anyone what to bring, or to bring anything at all. The perfect meal walked in the door, because the menu was a list of cherished names. Who was at the table? My wonderful friends, the ones who love to argue about wine and forget the argument after the first sip, who love to laugh and tell stories, who will stay up late, all crowded together now around my big table in the corner of the studio.

Six months of construction became three years. It didn't matter. My bohemian moment in the studio gave birth to the soup life, to a new book, and to a new perfect meal — the one that created itself. Because what mattered most was who was at the table.

Originally from Australia, award-winning chef **Skye Gyngell** worked at a number of Sydney's culinary institutions, at The French House and The Dorchester (with Anton Mossiman) in London, and as a chef to such high-profile private clients as Madonna and Mario Testino. A phenomenal reception to her work at Petersham Nurseries Café has led to her being compared to the legendary cook Alice Waters. She is the author of two highly acclaimed cookbooks, *A Year in My Kitchen* and *My Favorite Ingredients*. She has written for *Vogue* and is the Sunday food writer for *The Independent*.

MEMORIES OF MEALS GONE BY

Skye Gyngell

My favorite time to eat in the whole world is late in the afternoon, as the day's light softens and turns to dusk — in the summertime when the weather is good — and the table is laid outside and friends and family are seated around. The air smells sweeter at this time of day; it is cooler, less intense, and the atmosphere is somehow more languid. There is no sense of time, the outside world seems further away, and a dreamlike state seems to linger in the air. When the wintertime comes and the table is laid indoors, it's good to have a fire in the hearth and candles lit as the light begins to fall quickly and a chill begins to descend. Summer, autumn, spring, or winter does not change my desire to eat one long meal at this special time. To savor it slowly, over several hours, is what appeals to me.

Consideration of the table setting is important. It should

be laid with care, for that creates a sense of thoughtfulness and celebration. Perfection is not what counts here; cutlery and crockery need not match, and it is not important whether you have the right glass for the wine. The spirit in which you come to cooking and entertaining is what is important. By choice I would much rather eat at home with friends, either at my house or theirs. On the whole, restaurants don't satisfy me in the same way, for it is less easy to eat, as quickly or slowly as you please, with your elbows on the table, helping yourself to a little more here or there. Time always seems to go by so fast these days, we rush from here to there — meeting deadlines, fighting traffic jams, and, if you are like me, often eating on the run. So to have time — time with friends and family — feels luxurious, almost decadent.

There are so many meals throughout my life that have become treasured memories that it is hard to choose just one. Perhaps it was the time when I was sixteen, taken by my parents to a restaurant whose name was Claude's, situated in the urban heart of Sydney. It was small, dark, and glamorous to me. There, for the first time, I ate bouillabaisse — the broth with thick slices of toasted baguette floating on the top, smeared with that very unctuous of things, *rouille,* a sauce of red chiles, garlic, and breadcrumbs that is burnt orange in color, warm rather than hot in flavor, stirred into the hot and heady broth made from the cooking liquid of the fish. This is what transcends this dish into something truly wonderful. Bouillabaisse without *rouille* would be unthinkable. It is followed by the fish, a combination of scorpion fish (known as *rascasse* in France), langoustine, and snapper, cooked in no more than water, with a touch of white and golden threads of saffron. For dessert we ate a pear and Armagnac tart. That was all that was offered on the menu that night. This sense of perfection and belief that just this one dish needed to be served, struck me so profoundly that in many ways it changed the course of my life — it was the first time that food really fascinated me and it was then that I began to cook. It was then that I really *wanted* to cook.

Then there was the lunch I had with my father in a small trattoria just outside of Florence where for dessert we had peaches — ripe, downy, and sweet — sitting on top of shaved ice. The air was pounding with heat and this seemed the most perfect thing in the world to eat. Once again, I was struck by the rightness of just one thing — one perfect ingredient, unfussed with — pure and perfect in its beauty. That was when my love of ingredients, eaten only in their season and grown close to home, first came to me and it has stayed with me ever since.

I was just seventeen and it was the first time I had been to Europe — it was a holiday that I spent with my father on my own, a whirlwind business trip for him to which he had allowed me to tag along. I spent the days largely wandering around on my own in Athens, Rome, and the south of France, entranced by the sights, sounds, and smells that surrounded me; they were so very different from the large, blistering, open spaces of where I had grown up — it was not long before I left Australia permanently and moved to Paris – but it was this trip with my father when, for the first time, I think my senses truly came alive and this day in particular has always stayed with me. My father died ten years ago and so I treasure this memory as much now as I treasured that meal on that day almost thirty years ago.

Another meal I would choose was the one I ate early last year in the summer, late in the afternoon in the garden of my closest friend. It was a day when both children and grandchildren as well as parents all cooked together, nothing fancy — clams with dried chiles and fennel, beetroot, mozzarella, and chard, plenty of crusty peasant-style bread, and mulberries picked from the very top of the tree located at the far end of the garden. This afternoon meal was with my friend, Rose Grey, who died earlier this year. She was a cook who influenced me perhaps more than any other — it was there that I experienced, perhaps for the hundredth time, generosity between cooks.

In all the years now that I have been cooking, I have time and time again experienced the warmth of fellow chefs and cooks — a willingness to share knowledge and exchange ideas. Some have become dear friends, others have passed through fleetingly but have nonetheless still left their indelible mark. My cooking is a culmination of all that I have learned from others: Their generosity is what has moved me forward and in times when I have felt tired and weary and dream of doing something else — at the moment it's gardening — their enthusiasm very often re-ignites the flame and I fall in love with our craft once again.

Tracey Ryder is a food and wine writer, cook, gardener, and co-founder of Edible Communities, Inc., a network of over sixty regional food magazines across the U.S. and Canada. At least once a week she can be found at the stove, stirring a pot of risotto for dinner. In addition, Ryder, along with Edible Communities co-founder, Carole Topalian, released their first book, *Edible: A Celebration of Local Foods,* in April 2010. *Edible* is a presentation of beautiful color photography, seasonal recipes, and profiles of local food heroes from communities across North America.

A FAVORITE MAGIC MEAL

Tracey Ryder

Oftentimes I am chided by my mother and significant other for buying kitchen gadgets, exotic pantry items, a piece of antique dishware that has special indentations for serving oysters, or the next odd-shaped piece of clay cookware I just can't live without. They do this because after moving into our Santa Fe home three years ago, when it took me a full week to unpack all of the kitchen boxes that were stacked, quite literally, to the ceiling, I made the following proclamation: "If I ever buy another thing for this kitchen, one of you must shoot me."

While I'm happy to report that I am still standing today (and without wounds), I can't honestly say that I have refrained entirely from purchasing new items for the kitchen, but I can say that I have grown to love cooking more meals that are simple and straightforward, and that I can make without the use of fancy gadgets and by using only a handful of seasonal ingredients.

These more basic meals have a special quality to them — their memory lingers long after the last dish is washed and put away, and they provide us with a level of satisfaction that is comforting because of their uncomplicated nature. These meals belong entirely to the realm of the "clean plate club" because they are devoured fully and rarely provide any leftovers. Ironically, their preparation calls for only a few basic tools and ingredients: a cutting board, sharp knife, a simple homemade stock, a handful of herbs, a seasonal vegetable, a heavy-bottomed pan — no special gadgets, fancy cookware, or exotic ingredients are needed at all. Since the pleasure we derive from these dishes is in exact opposite proportion to the amount of work (or equipment) required, we consider them to be somewhat magical.

Our very favorite "magic" dish is risotto. This deliciously creamy rice and stock combination is infinitely adaptable by adding whatever fresh ingredient is in season — peas or asparagus in spring, cherry tomatoes or corn kernels in summer, wild mushrooms or a hearty squash in the fall, a seasonal fish. It's hard to think of something that would not work in tandem with a basic risotto, so it allows you to use your imagination and to try new combinations all the time.

It is said that the history of risotto goes back to the fourteenth century B.C., when the Arabs arrived in Sicily, bringing rice with them. Many Italian legends talk about the evolution of various risotto dishes over time but given the number of great Italian cooks who have made it over the centuries, I'm sure there are more variations than anyone can count.

The first time I tried risotto in a restaurant was about twenty years ago. The dish I had that evening was something close to divine — the aroma of sweet lobster meat and wild mushrooms wafted out of the steamy dish and I ate it wholeheartedly, taking very few breaks in between bites. As often happens for those of us who love to cook, we eat a dish like that in a restaurant and then race home to try and duplicate it.

I went into my first homemade batch with a lot of reluctance and fear of failure because I had heard that it was difficult to make, required an inordinate amount of time for stirring, and could easily become too gooey (from overcooking) or too *al dente* (from undercooking). And since the dish I had eaten in that restaurant was so utterly delicious, I felt certain it would be difficult to make. With no real recipe to follow (except for the bits of info pulled out of the waiter who had served the risotto to me), I had no idea what the right amount of stirring was or how to achieve the creaminess I had experienced the night before, but forged ahead nonetheless. That first result was nowhere near as complicated as I feared it might be and was so delicious it became a standard in our weekly repertoire of meals. And while it does require a good amount of stirring to make a tasty risotto, the process is so meditative, it actually relaxes you while you make it.

Another wonderful aspect of this dish is that it's the perfect one-dish meal. It is also inexpensive, highly adaptable to the season, and vegetarian friends love it for being a main course that is so hearty and satisfying, and gluten-free.

There is something romantic about risotto, too. Standing over the stove and stirring it while having a glass of wine and talking with friends has the ability to dissolve stress. The simple act of stirring, convivial conversations with friends, and a deliciously comforting dish everyone enjoys — now that is a meal you can love!

"MAGIC" SEASONAL RISOTTO

Serves 2 as a main course or 4 as a side dish

4 cups homemade vegetable or chicken stock (or good quality store-bought if you don't have homemade)

4 to 6 ounces shelled fresh peas or asparagus, bottoms trimmed and remaining stalks cut into 1-inch pieces (or wild mushrooms, dark leafy greens, or roasted butternut squash, depending on the season)

3 tablespoons extra virgin olive oil

1 medium shallot, minced

1½ cups of Arborio or Carnaroli rice (these are short-grained rice varieties that can absorb all of the stock without becoming overcooked)

½ cup dry white wine

6 sprigs fresh Italian parsley (optional), minced

1 tablespoon butter

½ cup finely grated Parmesan cheese

Salt and freshly ground black pepper

Heat the stock until hot but not boiling in a heavy-bottomed saucepan large enough to allow you to place a mesh strainer over the top of it so that the fresh vegetables you are using, either peas or asparagus, can begin to cook in the heated liquid as you cook the rice in another pan. Leave them in the hot liquid until they are tender but not fully cooked. The vegetables should remain in the strainer during this process.

Place a 10- to 12-inch sauté pan over medium heat, add the olive oil and shallot, and cook until the shallot's translucent and soft but not brown. Add the rice and cook while stirring constantly until each grain is coated with olive oil, about a minute. Add ½ cup wine and stir constantly until it is incorporated into the mixture.

Once the wine has been absorbed into the rice, begin adding stock to the pan, one ladle at a time, stirring constantly until each addition has been absorbed into the rice and a wooden spoon pulled through the pan leaves a trail behind it. Continue adding stock, one ladle at a time, and keep stirring in a steady circular motion until the rice is tender and creamy.

Once the rice is cooked and the mixture looks creamy, turn off the heat and add the parsley (if using), butter, and Parmesan cheese. Stir until all the ingredients are fully incorporated into the dish and the butter and cheese have completely melted. Add the peas or asparagus, or whatever other vegetable you are using, folding them thoroughly into the rice mixture. Add salt and pepper to taste. Serve hot in pre-warmed bowls.

Originally from the Deep South, Paris-based food writer **Wendy Lyn** knows the city's food culture inside and out. Although she has served as a culinary public relations advisor and friend to some of the best French chefs and restaurants in the world (Charlie Trotter, Alain Ducasse, Guy Savoy, and the red *Michelin Guide*), she remains a down-to-earth Southern gal at heart. Today she reports on the culinary scene in Paris as the founder/editor of The Paris Kitchen™ Web site and is the co-founder of the Paris Supper Club. In between deadlines, she leads food and wine walks for visitors looking to nibble and sip their way like locals through her little black book of insider culinary addresses.

LESSONS FROM PAPA

Wendy Lyn

Having traveled and eaten all over the globe, working with some of the best chefs and restaurants in the world, I'm often asked which city and chef's restaurant has inspired/taught me the most. That's an easy one . . . it was my grandfather (known as "Papa") and his kitchen.

His kitchen was more than a room in a house overlooking St. Andrews Bay in the Panhandle of Florida. "Kitchen" was a philosophy of learning life lessons through food and nature. He was my teacher, our classroom was the outdoors, my homework was working with the folks who fished and farmed, and my desk was his dining table.

To understand why Papa's philosophy made an impact on the meals I create and orchestrate, it is important to know that his outlook was formed at a very early age. His father, Oscar — a tough character born at the turn of the century — helped build one of the first railroads through the forests of Georgia to the coast of Florida. Instead of being a family man, he preferred women, drink, and gambling (he ran a profitable underground Prohibition-era establishment and once lost fifty miles of pristine sugar-white sand on the Gulf of Mexico shoreline in a single hand of poker because it was good for "nothing but growing potatoes" — this was before condominium was even a word). Oscar ended up running away, leaving the family penniless and my grandfather to step in as man of the house to take care of his mother and his seven siblings.

Since their house sat on a small plot of land, chicken coops were built and vegetable gardens planted. St. Andrews Bay (which empties into the Gulf of Mexico) was also a few blocks away and it was here that, as a young boy, Papa learned to harvest the bay's resources and till the land to feed the family. In true Huckleberry Finn-style, Papa was up before daybreak, rowing out into the bay, throwing a net to catch bait so he could then catch fish before gathering eggs in the yard, pulling up vegetables, shelling peas, cooking fruit to preserve jam, etc., all before he went to school. The kitchen was run like clockwork, organized into stations for prep and cooking, and the dining table was a place where his family gathered to count their blessings and break bread.

Papa went on to join the Navy, still supporting the family and doing what he loved best — serving people around a table as the ship's cook — and when he came back he married my grandmother, who had grown up in similar tough circumstances.

I didn't know that we were poor (electricity was expensive so most of our meals were cooked over a fireplace and illuminated by hurricane oil lanterns). I only knew that we were "rich" during our family meals when all Papa's siblings brought their children and their children's children to dine. I didn't have a clue that a meal for twenty people wasn't the norm for everyone else.

The table was always piled high with crispy buttermilk fried chicken, meatloaf, brown rice 'n' onions, macaroni and cheese casserole, cornbread and buttermilk biscuits served in cast-iron skillets, platters of fried shrimp and mullet caught that morning, and sides of turnip and collard greens just pulled from the garden and flavored with country ham, all of it washed down with pitchers of Grandma's fabulous sweet, sweet tea.

The turning point for me was when I was ten. Grandma shared what she thought was a funny story about the day when the pet chicken, "Penny," wasn't anywhere to be found;

laughing, she said that it was Papa who gave the news while carving the bird. I was horrified and inconsolable. Papa was upset with himself — he had only wanted to protect me from the hard work he had known but only then did he realize that he had also left me ignorant to the realities of where our food came from.

It was then that the Saturday culinary adventures started.

Papa would pick me up at 4:00 a.m., swearing me to secrecy over our agenda. I usually couldn't sleep the night before because I was so excited, and I would sit on the porch, ready to go, an hour early. We told my mom that we were going on "secret errands" — which really involved Papa teaching me to drive illegally on back country roads so we could meet and work with his farmer friends before driving to the docks to buy shrimp-crabs-fish direct off of the boats at the marina.

Every food adventure had a lesson in it but Papa had his hands full with a little blonde-haired, blue-eyed princess.

On a Forrest Gump-style boat at the marina, we went below and Papa handed me tongs to pick out crabs for lunch. I fainted at the sight of a big laundry basket crawling with squirming crabs trying to break free. When I came to, he handed me the tongs again saying, "If you want it, you are the only one to go get it, no one is going to hand you what you want."

While "gigging" flounder at midnight on a skiff in the mudflats with a flashlight, I'd complain about the hour and Papa would say, "Wendy, when you're looking for something you need, what difference does it make what time it is?"

On another princess occasion, I gasped in horror when Papa sat me on a stool under a goat to get its milk and said, "What we need doesn't always come from the obvious sources. Milk is milk." Standing on the jetty rocks in the Gulf of Mexico at sunrise, we'd cast for redfish and I'd grumble about not having had breakfast. Papa would reply pensively, "If you can get up before breakfast to catch lunch, then you'll really appreciate being hungry."

When I tried to open an oyster by banging it on the dock, he put it in my hand and showed me how to use a knife to pry it open, saying, "Always be gentle but firm." And so it went: Snorkeling for scallops meant I had to take a deep breath and hold it until I got what I was going after; wading the shorelines with a crab net taught me to keep my eyes focused on what I want or it might get away.

We even made the local news when we were up early walking the bay shores and ran smack into a huge, very dead beached whale. The authorities were notified and when the tractors came, Papa took me by the hand as we headed towards home and he said, "What is left behind is just as important as what was lived."

This made going to my actual school tough for me, because I couldn't understand what life lessons I was supposed to get from subjects like math and chemistry. As soon as the last bell rang I was driving to Papa's to roll up my pant legs and scavenge the shoreline to see what I could find, and then I'd scramble up to the kitchen to show him what I'd found . . . this was the "school learning" I loved best.

This upbringing became a way of thinking and living — and even now, thirty years later, living as a food writer in Paris, I can see a lesson in everything related to food and I love to have people laughing and enjoying a meal around the table.

My early days in a foreign country weren't easy and there were plenty of times I simply wanted to give up. Fresh off of the "turnip truck" from college in Birmingham, Alabama, and totally lost in translation, I landed in Paris feeling isolated for the first time in my life. I could see, but I felt deaf and mute because I couldn't understand the language, and I was ignorant to the ways of the Parisian French.

I ordered filet mignon but got pork (pork is *filet mignon* in France, not beef) and when I recognized the word artichoke on a menu, they might as well have handed me a pineapple with a knife and fork . . . in the South, artichoke is a dip served during the SEC championship playoff.

I was almost out of money and so lonely that I went to bed hungry, crying myself to sleep every night. Papa's gentle voice woke me from dreams saying, *"If you want it, you are the only one to go get it, no one is going to just hand you what you want."* So I'd rise, get dressed, and be out exploring the streets before most people were up, observing the rhythm of the city when the delivery trucks unloaded milk and vegetables. I was suddenly renewed and energized by all the activity before sunrise and I'd hear Papa's voice deep within me . . . *"If you can get up before breakfast to catch lunch, then you'll really appreciate being hungry."* Et voilà . . . I stopped wasting money on bistros and started shopping at the markets and cooking. Trying to talk to the food vendors must have seemed like an *I Love Lucy* episode but it forced me to get out and try to speak — to understand not just the language but the context in which words were spoken and the situations where they were used.

Call it luck, fate, or having become hand-gesture fluent . . . eventually, I found myself standing in the Poilâne bakery (not having a clue it was the bakery that was once a monastery in the seventeenth century) and trying very hard to ask questions about the big round wheels of bread that

I'd never seen before and why they didn't sell baguettes. The owner, Lionel, just happened to be there and spoke fluent English. Before I knew it, I was downstairs with him and a baker getting a deep philosophical lesson about the living qualities of handmade artisanal bread — soaking in these precious moments where I actually understood something that was going on. (Lionel once asked me to close my eyes and "listen" to bread being made — I thought it was a bit odd but when I did . . . there it was . . . a mixer whirring stone-ground flour, water, and sea salt together, heavy dough being kneaded on a floured wooden table, a heavy thud as the perfect amount was weighed on an old-time balance and scale, wooden paddles sliding in and out of the wood-burning oven, depositing bread, and the heavy clang of the oven door being lowered and shut. Lionel said, "Wendy, when all the different parts come together in a perfect rhythm, it is like music and when you close your eyes you can hear it, *non*? The symphony of life. It breathes and lives within us . . ."

Lionel was key in encouraging me to reach out to other Parisians who worked in food and wine. Looking back now, I have so many people in Paris that I am blessed to know and call family — and I might not have appreciated all they had to offer had it not been for the outings with Papa. He got me ready for the biggest food adventure of my life.

Coming full circle from Papa to Paris, these folks not only shared their passion and stories but taught me valuable life lessons on this side of the pond.

Chocolate maker Robert Linxe of Mason du Chocolat taught me the nuances of cacao and that finding your passion at fifty is better than never finding it. Restaurateur Drew Harre taught me about wood-fired oven breads and that the only thing better than being able to tell a good story is actually having lived it. Lionel's daughter, Apollonia, continued to educate me about bread after her father's untimely death, and wine aficionado Juan Sanchez introduced me to organic/small production winemakers in all regions of France. Both Apollonia and Juan reminded me through their own examples that living a 360° life outside work is essential to one's balance and well-being.

Finally, it was Michelin-starred chef Guy Savoy who showed me the ways of the artichoke (his black truffle artichoke soup remains my favorite dish to this day) and who taught me that no matter how big of a rock star you might be, you should never forget where you come from and you should always thank the people that helped you get to where you are.

Perhaps it was for that reason that I turned to Guy when Papa died. I was too devastated to go home for the funeral and kept my feelings to myself. I walked over to the restaurant for a bowl of soup. When he asked me what I thought of it I was just being polite when I said, "Oh, it's fabulous, Chef!" He looked at me and questioned, "But Wendy, you are telling me what you want me to hear — don't you want to know what went into making this dish? Where the products came from, who cared for them, and how they are prepared? This is very important in understanding food."

Before I left, he gave me a DVD he'd made with a big film company, and asked me to come back and taste the soup again after I'd watched it.

In the film, Guy lives out his own advice of never forgetting where you come from or the people who helped you get to where you are . . . I watched in awe as he visited all his producers on their farms and marine basins during all four seasons of the year — I felt he was personally taking me on a behind-the-scenes culinary journey into these folks' lives, homes, barns, fields, and boats.

He walked and sometimes hiked miles "in their shoes" to personally understand everything that went into the products of theirs that he uses in the restaurant. Guy made cheese in a one-room farmhouse, pulled up oysters from their ocean beds, hand-fed Bresse chickens in the dark, hauled sacks of walnuts to be crushed into oil, trailed a wheat farmer in his fields, and, along the way, really listened to them with all his senses.

It is ironic that on the day Papa left, I sat in Paris going on culinary adventures with my friend Chef Guy Savoy. The torch had been passed.

The film shows how at the end of the year, Guy invited all of the farmers, winemakers, and other food producers to his restaurant and cooked just for them, using only their products. Some of them had never before seen the outcome of their products nor been to Paris, let alone dined in a temple of gastronomy. And here they were, farmers wearing pullovers and jeans, sitting next to the winemaker of Château d'Yquem, sharing knowledge and breaking bread as equals.

Back in the restaurant a few days later with the black truffle artichoke soup in front of me again, I choked back tears and put the spoon down before I could even taste it. Guy smiled, "Now you understand . . . food is more than ingredients. It is a combination of history, emotion, craft, and tradition. What is in front of you is anxious to reveal all of this . . ."

Creating and orchestrating a meal I love goes back to the

core life lessons that Papa, Robert, Lionel, Apollonia, Juan, Drew, and Guy taught me — abundance, generosity, learning, teaching, giving back what you've been given, knowing where your food comes from, sharing it with those you care about and love, and never forgetting where you come from.

Today the city of Paris is my office, its passionate bakers, chefs, and artisans are my classroom, my homework is continuing to learn what they have to teach, and my desk is the table around which everyone in my life can share a meal that's made with all the lessons I've learned — and with love, too.

Karen J. Coates, an American journalist and author, covers food, environment, and social issues for publications around the world. She's a correspondent for *Archaeology* magazine and writes a food culture column for *The Faster Times*. She was *Gourmet's* Asia correspondent until the magazine closed in 2009. She is a 2010-2011 Ted Scripps Fellow in Environmental Journalism at the University of Colorado at Boulder. Karen and her husband, photographer Jerry Redfern, split their time between travels abroad and their home in New Mexico's Rio Grande Valley. You can get another taste of her writing on her food blog, Rambling Spoon.

THE LAST SUPPER

Karen J. Coates

The last supper: what would it be? If you had to choose, what would you eat? It's a common question asked of anyone whose heart resides in the kitchen — or anyone on death row. But how could I possibly pick one last dish to culminate them all?

In the end, I think, food is not nearly as critical as context.

Gasp! I hear murmurs of disbelief! But think back through time — the most memorable meals, the sweetest treats, the most succulent meats. Were they not packaged with people?

My last supper would resemble a marathon more than a single meal. I ask my husband, Jerry, to build us an exceptionally long table that stretches as far as my life is long. And I fill that enormous table with the histories and dishes of people I have known around the world. Then I invite all of our friends, and all of our family, and all of the cooks who have shaped me through the art of their kitchens. They share their stories, their cultures. They eat and chat, and everyone is fed equally on words and food.

We place that table on a warm summer day, high on a hilltop overlooking Waterton Lake, with a view toward Montana from its perch in Alberta. A small breeze ruffles the trees as cobalt waters hug the shore. Jerry disagrees (he thinks we should dine in our backyard), but I think this hill, overlooking this lake surrounded by these mountains, is one of the most beautiful places I have ever seen. And there is no better appetizer than beauty.

We eat and drink and talk for hours, with the warm sun on our backs. We have spicy *laap* with minced fish and roasted eggplant and plenty of dill from Louis's little Luang Prabang restaurant on the high banks of the Mekong River in Laos. We shape our sticky rice into little balls and lap up his fragrant salad as Louis tells us how he taught himself to cook. We munch on crispy sheets of Mekong riverweed, dried and fried, coated with sesame and chile, and dipped into sweet-spicy chile jam with buffalo skin.

We slurp through bowls of *bun cha,* just as I ate it at a little stall in Hanoi — cold noodles with a heap of fresh herbs, a tangy broth, grilled pork, tiny burgers, and the crispiest crab spring rolls. It takes some hunting, but I find Minh, Minh, and Linh — my trio of Vietnamese friends — and we eat *bun cha* together again while discussing our dreams for the future.

We have beef tacos with homemade tortillas and pico de gallo from the little village near Puerto Vallarta, where my cousin introduced my family to her friends and their food. We quench our thirst with bright crimson glasses of hibiscus, the same juice we drank that day in Mexico.

The entire table sinks into a platter of fish, grilled to a crisp, its flesh dunked into a tangy bowl of shaved green mango with garlic, lime, and chile — just as Sinith's family served it for Khmer New Year when Jerry and I first lived in Phnom Penh. Sinith, no doubt, strums his guitar and serenades the crowd with his soft rendition of "Unchained Melody." (It's just a little something Sinith does for his friends.)

I attempt to recreate the creamy salmon chowder Jerry and I ate on a blustery August night in Anchorage during our Alaskan honeymoon. And if I could, I would cover the hills in blueberries, just as we found them in Denali, so that each guest could traipse through the fields, filling — then emptying — one Nalgene bottle after another, with our fingers smeared, pantlegs stained, chins dripping in juicy purple goodness.

One end of the table is reserved for sushi, just as Masaru and Youme serve it in their Bangkok home with trays of fresh sashimi and perfectly seasoned rice. And every bite is accompanied with talk of photography and news, and the important issues linking all of us around this table, around the world.

I invite the Pa-O villagers in Shan State and ask them to make their green beans with peanuts and shallots. And we continue our conversations about airplanes and terrorism, potty-training babies, and growing food.

I invite all my Burmese friends for bowls of *mohinga* (fish broth with rice noodles), plates of pickled tea, and all the dishes they've offered to serve me — one day, someday, when the generals let me into their country again. We gather at this table and clink our glasses to Burma's future, as we have too many times now without change.

Walter supplies the table with luscious, drippy slices of his pineapple from his hillside in the Kelabit Highlands of Borneo. And I ask him to fry a batch of ginger flowers, plump and pink, so that everyone can ingest their fragrance. And he will bring his homegrown mountain rice, too. Organic, of course. It tastes as fresh as dew, or morning rain.

The air smells of pig, of brother-in-law Tom's melt-in-the-mouth, fall-off-the-bone *cochinita pibil*, pit-roasted pork wrapped in banana leaves and served with tortillas and an array of Tom's own salsas, from tomatillo to achiote.

We have a goulash-gulyas duet performed by two distinctly different mothers with two distinctly different versions of the same basic stew with the same Austro-Hungarian roots.

Val, our personal sommelier with an expert nose, chooses

the wine — and assures that every glass is eternally full. Her husband, Jon, contributes his forty-clove garlic chicken (and I might just stick my fingers straight into that madness).

I bring a few friends from Nagaland, and they bring a few of their chiles. I dare anyone at this table to taste a pinch of the world's hottest Naga pepper, which hits more than 1 million on the Scoville Heat Scale. Locals call it *raja,* meaning "king." With teary eyes and woozy heads, we listen to the Naga farmers explain how this chile cures their tummy troubles.

Jerry supplies his curry burgers, grilled over mesquite in a perfect mingling of Asian and Western flavors (see the recipe on page 187). I roast a Hmong chicken, using the recipe from Sami Scripter's and Sheng Yang's book, *Cooking from the Heart: The Hmong Kitchen in America.* It's the whole bird, bathed in coconut and stuffed with fish sauce, peanuts, mint, cilantro, and scallions. We have Hmong guests from Laos and Wisconsin, gathered for the first time since war disrupted their lives and flattened their homes.

This table goes on and on and on; so do the people, so do the foods. We have Cheng's pickles — just cucumbers marinated in saltwater with garlic, black pepper, and dill, as Cheng taught Jerry to do in Phnom Penh. We have Mrs. Lee's candied walnuts, smoked whitefish from Wagner's, and garlic cheese curds from Brennan's.

If I could, I would bring the king of Boti back to life. The princess cooks the simple, organic foods of this tiny Indonesian kingdom — spinach, popcorn, rice, all served in coconut bowls. Afterward, the royal court dances to gamelan music, the way the ancestors did upon returning home from war.

For dessert, sister-in-law Joanna offers an array of homemade ice creams and sorbets. But she competes with a special batch of black sesame from iberry, Bangkok's legendary ice cream institution. Jerry and I order nine cakes from Tomaselli's Pastry Mill in Oregon, just as we did for our wedding — chocolate and cheese galore. I ask Didier Corlou to make his crème brûlée with its pure texture of silk.

For those who prefer to drink their dessert: a bottle of sweet Riesling from Richard Sommer, father of Oregon wine, may he rest in peace. He's out there somewhere, watching this meal and nodding in agreement.

By now, we need a little perk: we drink silver-tip tea from the pickers we met in Sri Lanka, and rich Costa Rican coffee from Coopeldos (roasted to just the right moment, before the beans turn bitter).

As evening draws closer, all of us, from all of our disparate corners in the world, watch the summer sun set over blue-green hills. A hawk soars above us, then bats emerge from their darkened dens.

I grab a sweater, and I light a few candles, and we nibble until every belly is full. We drink until every thirst is quenched. And we talk until this table has no strangers — nor unfamiliar foods.

JERRY REDFERN'S SOUTHEAST ASIAN CURRY BURGERS *Serves 4*

1 pound high-quality grass-fed ground beef

2 to 3 stalks fresh lemongrass, coarse outer leaves removed and thinly sliced

1 large chunk of ginger, peeled and coarsely chopped

2 to 3 dried ancho chiles

1 teaspoon powdered turmeric or 1 small chunk fresh turmeric, peeled

1 teaspoon black peppercorns

1 teaspoon whole coriander

1 teaspoon cumin seeds

½ head garlic, cloves peeled

3 small shallots, roughly chopped

Drizzle of Asian fish sauce

Dollop of butter or ghee (optional)

Using a mortar and pestle, pound lemongrass, ginger, chiles, turmeric, peppercorns, coriander, cumin, garlic, and shallots until the mixture turns into a rough paste (a food processor will save time, but a mortar and pestle will coax more flavor from the ingredients). Mix the paste with meat and fish sauce, and form into small patties. Grill over an open flame. Good meat is key to recreating Asian flavors. Grass-fed beef will be lean. Try adding a dollop of butter or ghee if you want super richness. Grill until the burgers are nicely charred and crispy (but not burnt) on the outside yet tender inside. Or try the recipe with ground pork for burgers reminiscent of a Lao breakfast I had one morning at the Luang Prabang bus station, of all places (Lao bus stations sell some of the tastiest foods.)

Raghavan Iyer, CCP, is an author, educator, consultant, and spokesperson. He wrote *Betty Crocker's Indian Home Cooking, The Turmeric Trail: Recipes and Memories from an Indian Childhood* (a 2003 James Beard Foundation Award Finalist for Best International Cookbook), and *660 Curries,* named among the top cookbooks for 2008 by National Public Radio, the *New York Times, Boston Globe,* and *Food & Wine,* among many others, and it was honored as the 2008 Best Asian Cookbook in the USA by World Gourmand Awards. He received the highly coveted 2004 IACP Award of Excellence (formerly the Julia Child Awards) for Cooking Teacher of the Year, and was a Finalist for a 2005 James Beard Journalism Award as a contributing writer for *EatingWell* magazine.

BRAHMIN SOUL FOOD: A FATHER'S ONE-WAY JOURNEY TO THE LIFE HEREAFTER

Raghavan Iyer

Among the south Indian Tamilian Brahmins, as is true in Hinduism, death is the culmination of the present life cycle with rebirth and reincarnation as the next phase. Many hope to break free from this cycle and attain *moksha,* spiritual release from the cycle of reincarnation. The journey of the soul as it leaves one body and reaches its next destination is an important one and ritual foods nourish that lonesome path. The Parsees wet the lips of the dead with the same haoma juice or pomegranate juice that they use to welcome the newborn. According to tradition. they leave the body at a structure known as the tower of silence for the vultures to consume, as they believe in not polluting the five elements created by God. Brahmins invoke the God of Fire one last time to cleanse the body from years of sin, the same God

189

that ushered them into the human world at birth. My father's death was no exception.

The thirteen-day journey had begun, his soul now rejuvenated upon release from a diseased body. My brother, who was the eldest son, placed grains of rice and black sesame seeds in my father's mouth and poured clarified butter over the body as he lit fire to the chest area close to the heart. The ashes from the cremation were collected the next morning in an earthen pot and dispersed in the Arabian Sea. My father's mother sat on the terrazzo floor in the room where he had slept, her body rocking to and fro in childless sorrow. The shadow cast from the flame of an oil lamp was pitifully warped; her frail eighty-two-year-old being shook with uncontrollable grief. It was unfair of him to have died when he was the one who should have been around to light her funeral pyre. She grieved for a son who bore harsh abuse from his father, a son who protected her from her husband and provided her a safe haven all his life, a son who loved her unconditionally, a son whom she could not save from cancerous harm.

We understood his soul would wander for nine days, looking for every excuse to stay back in this world. The only guidance we could provide was a small cotton wick that we dipped in oil and kept lit; we never allowed the oil to dissipate, as we knew we must keep the flame alive. Merely two rice balls were placed out on the verandah for his soul's sustenance for the next nine days.

The *vadiyaars* (priests) came on the tenth day and offered the soul an elaborate meal without salt. The soul, angry at the tasteless food, hungry from the nine days of near starvation, was nudged to consider joining its ancestors as the rituals and Sanskrit verses filled the soul and our lives with purpose. The eleventh day, a single priest arrived and cooked his own meal in our kitchen with ingredients we furnished him, nurturing his body and my father's restless soul for one last satisfying meal.

The twelfth day was the most important one for the soul as it prepared to join its ancestors. The kitchen fires were lit and the women busied themselves with roasting and grinding spice blends never used in everyday cooking. Legumes used for festive celebrations, like yellow split peas and split and skinned black lentils, were put away while split and skinned green lentils took their place.

Soon the air was filled with the sweetness of sesame seeds toasted golden brown, pungent peppercorns, nutty roasted uncooked rice, and fresh curry leaves. Turmeric, a spice used every day in our Tamilian kitchen and a ceremonial symbol of my mother's marriage to my father, was markedly absent.

Arid rice husks, sweet-smelling, sun-dried dung cakes, ghee, and sprigs of *tulsi* (aromatic, sharp-edged leaves of holy basil) stoked the flames as offerings to the Hindu god Agni. Three priests sat around the fire, one representing my father's soul, the second his father, and the third his grandfather. The priest representing my father's soul was handed an umbrella, slippers, a hand fan, a bell to symbolize a cow, a water urn, pepper-spiked buttermilk, and cloyingly sweet jaggery (unrefined sugar), essential gear and sustenance for the spirit's one-way passage to the life hereafter.

At this juncture my mother was brought into the ceremonial circle, aware of the impending actions. Her wailing erupted from the pit of her soul and oozed from her sobbing throat. My aunt stood by her side as she raised her palm and wiped off my mother's sun-like *bindi,* her third eye, deep red and husband-blessed, now disappearing into the horizon, in companionship with my father's soul. Her *mangalsutra,* the 24-carat gold amulet that hung around her neck at the end of a turmeric-stained thread, first tied by her husband during their wedding, was now yanked and handed over to the priest. Her bangles were removed, one at a time, stripping her of her marital dignity. She stood her ground, short and defeated, simply dressed in a plain-colored saree, all alone, disrobed of her wifely role.

As prescribed by tradition, on the thirteenth day, my father reached his destination, a soul completely unbound from earthly desires, and fully prepared for a fresh beginning as he had finally attained *moksha*. At last, he was freed from reincarnation for being born a Brahmin and having lived a good life. Friends and family stopped by as we dressed in new clothes and welcomed them with a feast normally served during weddings and joyous occasions.

I sat cross-legged on the same spot as had the priest that represented my father two days ago. The chilled floor offered no comfort for the sorrow but the scent of a banana leaf in front of me, with a sprinkling of holy water to wipe it a shiny green, caused a rumble in my belly. The drizzle of clarified butter on one corner of the leaf ritually purified it. An array of snacks and condiments dotted the top half of the leaf: fresh fried plantain chips candied with jaggery, minced fresh turmeric pickled with ground red pepper and roasted mustard seeds, pigeon pea fritters studded with yellow split peas, fresh curry leaves, and dried red chiles, and a small mound of coarse sea salt. The offering of coconut-smothered stir-fries and saucy curries ensued, delectable combinations that proved Indians are masters at teasing vibrant flavors from vegetables like plantains, potatoes, summer squash, and spinach. A dollop of yogurt swirled with chile-stewed tomatoes, placed on the right hand corner just above the leaf's rib, completed that section's palette of flavors, colors, and textures.

The lower half of the leaf was yet to be addressed. Within seconds, a heap of perfectly cooked, steaming kernels of white rice took center stage, with a cavern molded on its top, volcano-like, an ideal home for stewed pigeon peas yellowed with turmeric and a liberal drizzle of clarified butter. A spoonful of dessert on the lower right corner of the leaf, a prelude to the final course, sweetened house-condensed milk blanketing creamy rice, promised a comforting finish. *Sambhar,* a delectable tamarind-based stew of seasonal root vegetables, redolent with roasted red chiles, legumes, coconut, and coriander, poured over the same pigeon pea-smothered rice, completed the mélange. My eager fingers reached for this savory delicacy that, at least momentarily, silenced the ache in my heart.

My father's soul now attained its final destination, perhaps taking solace in the knowledge that the loved ones he left behind were satiated with his lingering love, familial gatherings, and nurturing foods. The thirteen days of mourning, remembrance, and rebirth were orchestrated to bring peace around my father's physical death and to help him exult in his life hereafter. At times when I question if it did, the flavors of that meal pepper my own soul and squelch all doubts, and I know full well that my spirit, too, shall make that one-way voyage with equal consolation.

While working as a busboy in New Jersey, **Michael Paley** was drawn to the thrill of the kitchen and went on to train at the Florida Culinary Institute. Upon graduation, he worked alongside esteemed names like Daniel Boulud and Drew Nieporent before becoming executive chef of Proof on Main at the 21c Museum Hotel in Louisville, Kentucky. Under Chef Paley, Proof on Main has received numerous accolades, like a "Top Dining" category score in *Condé Nast Traveler;* and recognition as one of the "Best New Restaurants of 2006" by *Esquire* magazine. Michael was named "Rising Star 2007" by *Restaurant Hospitality* and has been featured in a number of publications, including *Food & Wine,* the *Wall Street Journal, Food Arts,* and the *New York Times.*

WHITE-APRON SYNDROME

Michael Paley

I'm sitting here asking myself if I'm the only person who cleans the kitchen *before* cooking.

It's Sunday, I just worked a six-day sixty-eight-hour workweek at the restaurant, and I want to cook a nice simple meal for my family.

But the kitchen isn't ready for me. Unfortunately, my wife has the equivalent of "white-coat syndrome" in the kitchen. It's true — when she sees raw meat, her hands get clammy, her pulse quickens, and she feels faint. Is there a term for that? Maybe "white-apron syndrome"... I like that, let's stick with that.

That being said, the kitchen is a bit disheveled. The range is dusty, my spices are unorganized, there are dishes in the dishwasher, and the stove is full of baking sheets and roasting pans. Don't feel bad for me, I am the one with OCD . . . or is it ADD?

Getting started on the right foot in the kitchen is essential. I feel one skill I have developed over the years, besides being able to cook good food, is the ability to be a good organizer. An organized chef, in an organized kitchen with an organized staff, can achieve great things, no matter what kind of cuisine you are trying to execute.

I am also a firm believer that cooking at home starts with the same building blocks — the best part being that you are alone, in your own space, designed by you with a pantry stocked by you. No banquets, no breakfast service, no wedding tastings . . . these are all things chefs *love* to do, but the more moving parts, the harder it is to drive the ship.

As a professional chef, I could easily say my favorite meal is one cooked by someone else. Sometimes we long for a break or to just mindlessly enjoy a meal without feeling any logistical attachment to it. It's not often we get to sit down and just eat.

The truth is, however, cooking at home for my family is the ultimate relaxation from a stressful week in the kitchen. It's just me, my cutting board, my Bose, my dull house knives, and a beer or glass of wine. These are the elements of a great meal. Maybe because some of the pressure is removed or that everything is being made in smaller, more personal amounts, I'm not sure. I just know that I can make a five-gallon batch of soup fifty times over the course of a few months at the restaurant and, while it tastes great, that same soup made at home always has something over it.

At home, I like to keep it simple. Just like in the restaurant, the most fun time to cook at home is summer when the farm is producing at its peak and the farmers' markets are in full swing. Heirloom tomatoes, fragrant herbs, fennel, eggplants, pole and runner beans all scream summer.

Almost every meal I cook at home during the summer starts with a plate of sliced heirloom tomatoes from Woodland Farm sprinkled with sea salt, shredded basil, and a Tuscan extra-virgin olive oil. Maybe a splash of vinegar, maybe not, depends on the variety of tomato.

I grew up in New Jersey and now live in Kentucky, two regions known for really good corn, so it is never forgotten at my table. My favorite variety grown locally is called Peaches and Cream. I love to throw it on the top rack of the grill in the husk to steam while the meats and sausages are grilling. Then we remove the husk, rub it with olive oil, salt, and pepper, and char it on the grill. Once off the grill, it gets the toppings of all toppings: pimenton aioli, grated pecorino, lime zest, and sea salt.

For the entrée, nothing beats a good Milanese. Pounded

chicken or pork — of course, I prefer pork — lightly breaded and pan-fried golden brown on both sides. I love to squeeze fresh lemon juice on it as it comes, still sizzling, out of the pan. The main ingredient in the garnishing salad is my favorite salad green, arugula, tossed with shaved onion, Sungold tomatoes, cucumbers, and shaved parmigiano. This makes the perfect meal.

For me it's not about the one meal that blew my mind, it's about that one or two or three times a month I get to cook at home. That is the kind of meal I remember, the kind of meal I cherish. It is not formal or organized. There is no pomp and circumstance. No courses, no matching china or stemware, no pretense. What is perfect is the place, the company, and the ingredients. And, if anything, it's a chance for a professional chef to relish the imperfection of something that seems so perfect and enjoy a meal with family.

Julee Rosso is the co-founder of the famed Silver Palate retail, catering, and manufacturing business. Her most recent book is *Fresh Start* and she is also the author of *Great Good Food* and the co-author of *The Silver Palate Cookbook* (inducted into the James Beard Cookbook Hall of Fame in 1992), *The Silver Palate Good Times Cookbook* (winner of the 1985 Duncan Hines/IACP Award for the Best Entertaining Cookbook), and *The New Basics Cookbook,* which together have over six million copies in print. Julee has appeared on numerous television and radio programs, including the *Today Show, Good Morning America,* and *20/20.* She was inducted into the Who's Who of American Food and Beverage by the James Beard Society. Since 1991, Julee, along with her husband, Bill Miller, has owned the acclaimed Wickwood Inn in the artist's community of Saugatuck, Michigan. Julee continues to lecture, conduct cooking classes, consult, and write.

AN ODE TO JULIA

Julee Rosso

"Life itself is the proper binge." — *Julia Child*

She crept into my life in 1968, slowly at first, until she became a dominant part of every week. For Julia taught me to cook — one recipe at a time — just as she has so many of us. I began at the beginning of *The French Chef,* and page by page discovered boeuf Bourguignon, coq au vin, puff pastry, daube, duxelles, naverin, blanquette, bourride, bouillabaisse, coquilles, omelettes, aioli, vacherin, mousse, soufflés, pot-au-feu, lobster Thermidor, croquembouche, and crêpes Suzette. It was easy, she was there. Can't you just hear her as she boomed out those melodic recipes' names? I can.

*"Admiring a chef and getting to know him is like loving
goose liver and then meeting the goose."*
— *Julia Child*

I finally met her twenty years later when she, her husband,

Paul, and I were sharing a "Loo" at Pat and Walter Wells's "Chanteduc" in Vaison en Romaine, Provence. About forty of us were there to celebrate Pat's birthday, but the joy for all of us was "hanging out" with Julia. Picking arugula, making ganache for the birthday cake, baking bread in the outdoor oven, and, of course, eating and drinking gloriously, all the while laughing!

During the course of the weekend Julia and I periodically discussed computers and that we'd never have to learn about them. Instead she quizzed me about *W*, a fashion publication I'd been very involved with. She wanted to know who all those New York society ladies were — each and every one. She warbled off their names and I was supposed to fill in their stories. Who would have thought Julia would ever be interested in that stuff? I soon learned that she was interested in everything and simply loved to gossip!

"I just love to eat!" — *Julia Child*

Back in New York, we had dinner quite often when she was in town. She always wanted to try the latest and greatest restaurants, and she always ate with great gusto — heaps and heaps! She loved good food! We worked together to enlarge the American Institute of Wine and Food, her energy knowing no bounds in her effort to legitimize the art of food and wine and the professionals who worked in the industry.

She cajoled and charmed, relentlessly, for donations to build the AIWF. Julia loved to win!

"Too few people understand a great cheese." — Julia Child

So full was her plate that she never knew what time it was. She'd call our home whenever — without hesitation — before 6:00 a.m. and well after midnight. Over the phone would come "JULEE!!!!" Yes, in capital letters. Now that wakes you up in a hurry! My husband, Bill, always knew when I had been speaking with Julia. There was a smile on my face that wouldn't go away and I'd have to tell him her latest. She loved to laugh! She called once when I was in New York. In asking for me, she said, "This is Julia Child," and Bill replied, "Oh, I'd never have known." "Oh quit!" she giggled. The girl loved to flirt!

"I was thirty-two when I started cooking. Up until then I just ate."
— Julia Child

One winter, my partner from The Silver Palate and I were being roasted by The New York Culinarians, and Julia, Irena Chalmers, Florence Fabricant, and Barbara Kafka were to do the deed. Wills and I were delayed by a snowstorm in Aspen and arrived one-and-a-half hours late for the dinner. We thought we'd sneak in and quietly take our seats for dinner. As we entered the room of four hundred, leaping up into the air, shouting, "Wills, oh, Wills, I must meet you at last," was Julia. Wills is my name for Bill and therefore that's what Julia called him . . . We are the only two people in the world who got away with that!

She came galloping amongst the tables, arms outstretched, heading straight for us, actually him! Everyone knew we had arrived! Wills instantly fell in love with her and her with him. My tall man loved that he had to look up at her. She loved men!

She always kept us in stitches, exaggerating about "hundreds of hours" of cooking time and "hundreds of cups" of stock. She kept asking me, "How many zillions of cookbooks have you sold, Julee?" as we sat side by side at various tables signing books. She wanted everyone to be successful!

The years flew, and I always wanted to do a "Julia and Julee" cooking class, there were so many stories we could tell. But, I could never ask her. She was always so immersed in serious endeavors for our industry and taking care of her dear, dear Paul. But, as *Julie and Julia* made my eyes overflow with memories for that simpler time, when the most important thing was whether the chocolate soufflé would really rise, I decided it's time. Here is a little cooking class . . . in a fashion . . .

JULIA'S LITTLE CHOCOLATE BITES *Yields 44-46 miniature bites* (*PETITE NUAGES DE CHOCOLATE*)

We've been a bit obsessed with these chocolate treasures for years and have kept them secret. They're bite-sized versions of Julia's Flourless Chocolate Cake, an idea she gave us long ago. Finally we've decided to share this embarrassingly simple recipe. Chocolate Bites have a crunchy top and beneath the consistency of a cloud. They simply dissolve into lovely silky chocolate in your mouth. Pace yourself. They're deceptively rich. We love these served still slightly warm, even if they crumble slightly, on a plate with a dollop of loosely whipped cream, or, if cooled, sprinkled lightly with confectioners' sugar.

9 ounces best quality bittersweet chocolate (60-64% cacao)

1 cup plus 2 tablespoons unsalted butter, cut into small pieces

1⅓ cups sugar

3 tablespoons all-purpose flour

5 large eggs, lightly beaten

Roughly chop the chocolate into pieces. Transfer to a medium-size bowl and add the butter. Place the bowl over a saucepan of simmering water until the two ingredients have melted. Mix well, transfer to a large bowl, and set aside.

Preheat the oven to 325°F. Sift the sugar and flour together, then stir into the chocolate. Add the eggs and mix well. Cover and let rest at room temperature for 30 minutes. The batter will thicken as it stands.

Place individual miniature silicone muffin cups on a large baking sheet. Spoon the mixture into the cups until full and slightly rounded on top. Bake for approximately 25 minutes, the until puffed and crisped on top. Remove from the oven and let cool completely in the muffin cups, if you can leave them alone, as they're fragile until cooled. Best within 24 hours, but still quite heavenly, if kept in an airtight container, for up to five days.

Marcus Samuelsson is chef/owner of Red Rooster Harlem in New York City. He was the youngest chef to ever receive two three-star ratings from the *New York Times,* and was honored by the James Beard Foundation as a "Rising Star Chef" (1999) and "Best Chef: New York City" (2003). His award-winning cookbooks include *New American Table* and *The Soul of A New Cuisine* (foreword by Desmond Tutu). Born in Ethiopia and raised in Sweden, Marcus was recognized by the World Economic Forum as one of the "Global Leaders of Tomorrow." In 2010, Marcus won Bravo's *Top Chef Masters* season 2 competition and has received four-star ratings in *Forbes* and was named one of the "Great Chefs of America" by the Culinary Institute of America.

MY FAVORITE SPAGHETTI RECIPE

Marcus Samuelsson

My mom's dad, Edwin Jönsson, didn't trust pasta. Born in 1901, he grew up in Sweden under very poor circumstances, and the poor man's cooking of his childhood dictated his palate for the rest of his life. He preferred the grease left over in the frying pan to butter, meatballs and meat loaf to steak, and he insisted on boiled potatoes with every meal. When the 1970s rolled around and trendy foods such as spaghetti with garlic started appearing, he thought it wasn't real food. (Don't even get me started on what he thought about rice.)

Spaghetti with meat sauce and peas was the one pasta dish that my mom made, and whenever my grandfather was there, she'd have to make him his own side dish of boiled potatoes. He spooned the meat sauce over the potatoes and ate them while we feasted on our noodles. I've adapted my mother's recipe, making the sauce lighter and fresher, and I use a healthier, whole grain pasta.

MY MOTHER'S SPAGHETTI WITH PEAS   *Serves 6*

1 pound whole wheat spaghetti

2 tablespoons olive oil

1½ cups peas

2 egg yolks

2 tablespoons grated Parmesan cheese

2 tablespoons heavy cream

½ cup diced pancetta

1 onion, chopped

3 garlic cloves, chopped

Zest of ½ lemon

1 tablespoon chopped parsley

6 basil leaves, torn

Salt

Freshly ground pepper

Bring a large pot of salted water to a boil. Add the spaghetti and simmer until *al dente*, about 8 minutes, or according to directions on package. Strain and toss with olive oil.

Prepare an ice bath by filling a bowl with water and ice cubes. In a small pot, bring 2 cups of water to a boil. Add the peas and simmer for 30 seconds. Remove the peas with a slotted spoon and transfer them to the ice bath to keep their fresh, bright green color.

Whisk together the egg yolks, Parmesan cheese, and cream. Set aside.

Heat a large sauté pan over low heat. Add the pancetta and sauté until crispy, about 8 minutes. Add the onion and garlic and sauté until translucent, another 4 minutes. Add the spaghetti and cook until heated through, about 4 minutes. Season with salt and pepper. Remove from heat and toss with the egg-Parmesan mixture and lemon zest. Garnish with parsley, basil, and peas and serve immediately.

This recipe is reprinted from *New American Table* by Marcus Samuelsson (Wiley). Used by permission of John Wiley & Sons Inc.

As executive pastry chef of New York's Le Bernardin, **Michael Laiskonis** produces delicate desserts that are a flavorful balance of art and science, both contemporary and classic. Awarded "Outstanding Pastry Chef" in 2007 by the James Beard Foundation, his work has also helped the restaurant maintain three stars from the esteemed *Michelin Guide* and four stars from the *New York Times*. Named by *Pastry Art and Design* as one of the "10 Best Pastry Chefs in America," Michael has been featured in numerous print, television, and radio appearances internationally. He was *Bon Appétit's* 2004 "Pastry Chef of the Year" and Starchefs.com declared him a "Rising Star" in 2006. He has advisory positions with the Institute of Culinary Education and Starbucks.

MY LIFE, MY MEAL

Michael Laiskonis

A love of food came to me relatively late. Sure, I have my share of pleasant associations with food from my childhood, but my upbringing was by no means one grounded in gastronomic pleasure. It wasn't until my early twenties, after falling into professional cooking by accident, that I began to explore a whole new world of flavor and culinary adventure. Ever since, most of the memorable moments in life as I know it have been marked by an intense encounter with food. Perhaps I see my life as, indeed, one long meal, a tasting menu that spans continents and evokes a wide range of emotions.

There are many elements that comprise a "perfect" meal beyond basic taste; it's often the far less tangible aspects that separate "dining" from merely "eating," and "pleasure" from "simple sustenance." Through food we create physical and emotional associations with a deeply rooted sense memory — a pleasant aroma, flavor, or texture can transport us back to a specific time and place, a state of mind, or sense of community. I consider myself lucky that my job as a chef gives me access to a great deal of culinary epiphany. The things I've eaten serve as documentation of experience, much like a photo album. My perfect meal just might be a composite of these nibbles and bites over a lifetime. These edible snapshots, woven together as a whole, tell a greater — and very personal — story.

℘ ℘ ℘

First Course: Sense of Place
Breakfast, Outside Tsukiji Fish Market, Tokyo, 7:00 a.m.
Lobster Bake, Nantucket Beach, Dusk

Food is often the easiest gateway through which we navigate new territory and access cultures different from our own — eating is a language we all speak. We can learn a lot about a place and its people by what they cultivate and, ultimately, by what they put in their stomachs. This idea of place — the setting and time — also offers an authenticity that is difficult to replicate anywhere else. It is the taste of a single moment. I tend to immediately peel away the sensory overload a new environment presents by searching for what the locals eat, their rituals and traditions. I would kick off my ideal meal with a course in two parts, beginning with a breakfast of noodles and slices of impeccably raw fish at a counter alongside the workers of Tokyo's Tsukiji Fish Market. I'd follow that with a much different sea-bound ritual: the smoky and salty flavors of lobster, clams, sausages, corn, and potatoes, slowly cooked in a hole dug on the beach of Nantucket, just feet away from the pounding surf.

చ్చ చ్చ చ్చ

Second Course: Discovery
Lechón, San Juan, Puerto Rico
Spicy Squid and Pig's Ear Stew, Market Stall, Bangkok

Few things are as exciting — or terrifying — as encounters with new and exotic foods, or those pieces and parts we've distanced ourselves from in the name of convenience. I was a picky eater growing up, and as an adult I tend to over-compensate by seeking out the rare and unusual. That first taste of something new is often the one we remember most. I think we regain a connection to where our food comes from when it's placed before us in nose-to-tail form. Cooking, and then eating, a whole animal is a lesson in responsibility, economy, and pure deliciousness.

My second course comes courtesy of chef and friend Alfredo Ayala in Puerto Rico, responsible for my first taste of lechón (whole, spit-roasted suckling pig). Best eaten without utensils but by hand, the rich flavors are expressed in a range of textures — impossibly crispy skin, moist flesh, and pockets of melting fat. Perhaps a side dish for this course might include a bowl of stew, with squid, pig's ear, and coagulated blood, served from a stall within one of Bangkok's dusty, sprawling markets. The spicy and gamey breakfast reflected the sights, sounds, and smells assaulting me as I browsed the winding alleyways filled with strange new ingredients.

ဢ ဢ ဢ

Third Course: Pilgrimage
The French Laundry, Yountville, California

Anticipation is an overlooked aspect of a meal. Spontaneity and the element of surprise have their places, but there are also those dinners that are planned well in advance. A great many of us plan whole trips around a visit to one grand temple of cuisine or another. Such a pilgrimage is usually weighed with unreasonably high expectations, but then exceeding those expectations is what such restaurants do. It's why they become destinations in and of themselves.

At the risk of being guilty of gluttony, I'd say my entire meal of seventeen courses at Thomas Keller's French Laundry would have to find a place on my perfect menu. Taken as a whole, it's rather difficult to single out this dish or that. Though the price is never small, it serves as admission to an entire experience, immersion into an overall atmosphere, a relinquishing of all control to a chef, if only for just a few hours.

 ✰ ✰ ✰

Fourth Course: Hunger
Christmas Eve Dinner, Detroit

There are those times when almost anything will taste good; hunger, in the end, is why we eat. In such cases satisfaction is simply a full belly. My fourth course is one such moment, some fifteen years ago, my first Christmas season as a young cook, in the "shit," as it were. I was a baker at a small outfit in the outlying suburbs of Detroit. We were producing around the clock for over two weeks. By Christmas Eve, it was all flying out of the shop as fast as we could fill the cases. I was feeling that deep, to-the-bone kind of tired, surviving only on what little adrenaline I could summon until we finally locked the doors at 4:00 p.m.

I had managed to grab one of the last unsold baguettes, and headed home, exhausted and hungry. On the long drive back to my rented flat in the city, I began to realize that most of the markets had closed as well. I had just enough at home to scrape together a simple pasta. Along with the bread I had made with my own hands, it was a simple solitary dinner, a quiet reward for a lot of hard work. A deeper hunger was satisfied, and it was an early lesson in just how good food could taste in context. And then I slept, well into the next day.

℘ ℘ ℘

Fifth Course: Rites of Passage
Skate Sautéed in Goose Fat with Squab Jus,
Le Bernardin, New York

Food acts as a celebratory focus of special occasions the world over, in every culture. In many ways, the longest-lasting memory of the event is the meal itself. One such pivotal moment marked the early years of my career as a cook. The chef I was training under was invited to cook at the storied James Beard House in New York, and of course I would come along to assist. The day after our successful dinner, we found ourselves at Le Bernardin for lunch. I still remember every bite of food from that lunch, from the salmon rillettes through to the warm chocolate tart.

I had one dish that, to this day, has remained especially memorable. The main course — fifth in my perfect menu — was skate, sautéed in goose fat, sauced with a squab jus. That single plate displayed a whole world of potential, justifying my passion to cook and clearing a path I continue down to this day. At that time, before the second floor of Le Bernardin had been remodeled to become the private dining rooms, the long hallway back to the restrooms revealed a large window looking into the kitchens. I must have lingered there for several minutes, mesmerized by the activity, the army of white-clad cooks. I never would have guessed I would one day be among them.

Ꮣ Ꮣ Ꮣ

Sixth Course: Conviviality
Street Food, Bangkok

One might say that good company can often make up for bad food, but great food will never compensate for poor company. What we're eating can be eclipsed by the atmosphere provided by the family and companions we share our meals with, or those we cook for, or those who cook for us. Time at a shared table is ideal for conversation and storytelling. Through the common denominator of food we connect emotionally to one another. I've had many memorable meals in the company of my colleagues, that is, with other chefs. As much as we analyze most things we eat, we often like to say that the best things to eat are those cooked by *other* people. Light-hearted banter will inevitably evolve into shop-talk; what could be better than doing what you love, while talking about it to other people who love what they do, too?

One such meal serves as my sixth course — less a meal, per se, but rather a "crawl" through the streets of Bangkok, with a half-dozen chefs. We had all come to Thailand from elsewhere — the U.S., Moscow, Iceland, and Italy — to cook together, and when the cooking for others was over, we then sought to feed ourselves. The progressive dinner began with noodles from one tiny storefront, followed by steaming bowls of meaty soup from another down the street. Into a couple of taxis, and moments later we were on another sidewalk, tucking into raw shrimps, whole fried fish, and giant curried crabs, all washed down with local beer. Most of my lasting friendships have formed at such meals, amidst swapping tales of kitchen chaos, sharing techniques, and professional gossip.

ɷ   ɷ   ɷ

Seventh Course: Dining Alone
Pierre Gagnaire and L'Arpège, Paris

Though company is an important aspect to the dining experience, it certainly isn't compulsory. Solo dining offers a unique experience, allowing one to take in the subtleties of food and service that might otherwise go unnoticed. Truth be told, those dining alone might actually receive the bonus of just a little bit more attention from the staff, a few extra bites from the kitchen. While the idea of a party of one might strike many as depressing, strange, or uncomfortable, those of us who make a regular practice of it do so, above all else, just for the food.

For a few years running, I was making regular visits to Paris, highlighted by a ritual of treating myself to a pair of solitary lunches: one afternoon at Pierre Gagnaire, the next, across the Seine at L'Arpège. The Michelin-starred meal is the apex of haute cuisine, enjoyed only by a lucky few, and often an experience I don't necessarily want to share! For course number seven, I might wish to combine the joy, mystery, and energy of Gagnaire's unique style of cooking with the cool elegance and refined pampering of Alain Passard's L'Arpège. Who knows, had I been joined by someone else, I may never have laughed out loud with happiness while working my way through Gagnaire's dish of tuna and foie gras, nor likely would I have been invited to finish my coffee and *petit fours* at a corner table, joining Passard himself as he enjoyed a simple lunch.

∾ ∾ ∾

Eighth Course: Nostalgia
Chocolate-Hazelnut Tart, wd-50, New York

As we grow into childhood, I think our lifelong tastes, preferences, and associations with food begin to crystallize. As with Proust's madeleine, it is often the sweet that becomes intertwined with memory, emotion, and a sense of comfort. Dessert functions as a reward for eating those vegetables, a miracle salve for that scraped knee, or even a mischievous child's stolen secret. Personal nostalgia will vary by culture, country, region, or generation; it can be triggered by a freshly baked pie like Grandma used to make, or it may come in the form of mass-produced junk food (I'm convinced that all pastry chefs have, consciously or not, tried to recreate a Snickers bar in some way or another). These associations remain through adulthood. For a pastry chef, playing to this inner child can initiate the creation of something new; the context of such nostalgia, especially unexpected in a fine dining environment, heightens such playfulness.

Known for pushing the contemporary culinary envelope, wd-50's chef/owner Wylie Dufresne skillfully turns the familiar and low-brow on its end, transforming pedestrian fare such as fried chicken or corned beef into avant-garde creations. But my eighth course marks a transition into dessert, pastry chef Alex Stupak's chocolate and hazelnut tart in particular. His style employs modern technique and complex architecture to enhance flavor. Though his "tart" isn't engineered in any conventional way, the deep flavors are cut ever so slightly with coconut, resulting in an ineffable flavor, a sense of nostalgic déjà vu. When I ate this dessert, the effect was haunting, and I still haven't quite figured out the source of that memory.

ℰℐℴ ℰℐℴ ℰℐℴ

Ninth Course: Inspiration
Pastry, Hotel Room, Paris

As a chef, much of what I seek out and eventually consume is done so in a strictly professional capacity. Research, if you will, is not only a continuous cataloging of techniques and ingredients, but also a conscious awareness of trends. Deconstructing a dish in such a manner is akin to an archeological dig, a patient removal and study of its components, always asking why or how its author did this or that and, importantly, how I might improve upon it myself. This analysis will eventually filter through my own training and sensibilities, expressing itself in some degree that may be unrecognizable (or not) from its source. I do feel that chefs must always taste and learn, or else they risk a sort of narrow-mindedness, a culinary and intellectual implosion.

My meal then continues with course nine, an assortment of pastry, dumped from bags onto the bed of a Paris hotel room. The haul is a morning's worth of browsing among the city's — if not the world's — best boulangeries, pâtisseries, and chocolatiers. This is serious business, assessing the latest *macaron* innovation from Pierre Hermé, shiny chocolate bonbons from Patrick Roger, or Sadaharu Aoki's French classics infused with the flavors of Japan, the aroma of green tea or black sesame. The haute pastry houses release seasonal collections much like fashion designers do; I'll survey the shop windows for the latest trendy flavors and cake designs, but I also scour the local supermarket for ingredients I just can't find at home. The resulting sugar high is, of course, all in the name of research!

ↁ ↁ ↁ

Tenth Course: Reflection
Blueberry Pie and Coffee, Cape Ann, Massachusetts

I'm a chef and I work a lot. Long hours, often six days a week, and my busiest time is when everyone else is at play. I've come to use food — I wouldn't always consider it a meal — as a diversion, an excuse to pause, a means of extracting myself from the kitchen if only for a few brief moments. Doing so allows for a break that might not present itself otherwise. The act of eating, or snacking on whatever is at hand , is not what's important. Rather it's all about the mental and physical rest, the internal realignment, that food can provide.

The conclusion to my ideal meal is a simple slice of blueberry pie, topped with a scoop of vanilla ice cream, alongside a cup of black coffee. I'm sitting with my wife, at a picnic table behind a roadside shack, overlooking a small cove on the Massachusetts coastline. It's a sunny August afternoon, and a lone lobsterman is dropping his traps in the shallows. The pie is fine, as is the coffee, but ultimately forgettable. In contrast with the detailed memories I've laid out, this moment is important precisely for what it *isn't*. Returning to New York City from a rare week's vacation in Maine, we could just as easily have stuck to the main highway, forever oblivious to this idyllic spot, the pie, and the lobsterman. Had we not sought out the diversion, we may have missed these few precious moments together, watching the world go by. And in the end, that time of quiet reflection is the most important element of a perfect meal.

Jonathan King is co-founder and co-owner with Jim Stott of the nationally acclaimed Stonewall Kitchen, award-winning manufacturer of the famous specialty food products under that brand name. Jonathan and Jim also own and operate a restaurant, a cooking school, and currently nine of their own retail stores along the East Coast. The Stonewall Kitchen headquarters in York, Maine, where the products are made, has become a major tourist destination with close to one-half million visitors annually. They are the co-authors, along with Kathy Gunst, of a number of Stonewall Kitchen cookbooks, including *Stonewall Kitchen Grilling,* which was named to *Publishers Weekly's* "top ten list of the season's most enticing guides to grilling." Jonathan and Jim's roots began with strong passions for horticulture and cuisine, and today they continue to raise their own vegetables, and enjoy canning, and experimenting with new products on the weekends.

A SUMMER'S HIDDEN GEM AND A WINTER'S FEAST

Jonathan King

When Ronnie Sellers, the publisher of this book, asked if I would contribute an essay about my most memorable meal, I agreed easily. It seemed, at the time, like a simple task. I was so thrilled to be helping Share Our Strength®, an organization that our company has supported for years, and is dear to my heart. As I began reminiscing about all the amazing meals I have experienced over the years, all the places I have visited, it was truly overwhelming. When it came down to it, I found it impossible to narrow it down to the *most* memorable ONE.

As co-founder with Jim Stott of Stonewall Kitchen, I have been so lucky to be surrounded by delicious foods and by friends and colleagues who equally share my passion for food. We don't just love good food or fine dining, we enjoy everything that goes along with it. The planning of the menu, shopping for just the right ingredients, the prep work, time spent leisurely cooking (usually with a glass of wine in hand), serving, and then watching our guests enjoy it all . . . that's what it's all about. When I thought about this and remembered all the dozens and dozens of good times shared with good friends and great food, I realized it wasn't really about the food — it was truly about the experience: the setting, the sights, the aromas, and, most importantly, the company.

We all know that even the simplest meals can be the most memorable ones when experienced in the perfect setting with great friends — whether it's a mid-week summer evening when you spontaneously invite a few close friends over for a quick dinner in the backyard and serve juicy hamburgers, perfectly grilled over smoky briquettes and topped with lots of melting blue cheese, with a creamy potato salad and ice cold beer, while watching an orangey-pink Maine sunset, or a simple green frisée salad with golden brown lardons (strips of fried pork bacon) topped with a perfectly poached egg and served with a crispy baguette and sweet butter eaten slowly at a small bistro table at one of the thousands of crowded Parisian sidewalk cafés. I could go on and on with stories of delicious meals, beautiful settings, and great company.

For example, there is a place called Chauncey Creek that's tucked away on a back cove in Kittery Point, just a few miles from our home in Maine where the traditional lobster dinner is elevated to the ultimate Down East experience. First off, the restaurant sits literally on a floating dock that hangs over a bone-chillingly cold creek just a few yards from where the lobstermen bring in their traps every day. After you hand-select your lobster from the saltwater tank, the chef steams (never boils) the lobster perfectly, and tanned college kids bring it to you at one of the brightly colored picnic tables on the dock along with all the basics you need — lobster crackers, a pick, fork, fresh lemons, hot melted butter, and, most important of all, a big plastic bib!

And now here is my favorite part about dining on this spectacular dock, and a locally known secret of this hidden gem: Diners can bring with them anything else they want for dinner (and locals know to never forget the bug spray!). It is so fun to check out all the tables laden with everything from paper plates, beer, and potato chips, to fine china, linen tablecloths and napkins, wine, and an occasional silver candelabrum. We usually tote along candles, a carefully pressed, white-linen tablecloth, our favorite plates, nice stemware, silverware, and always a vase of flowers freshly cut from our home gardens. We usually start with glasses of wine served with a selection of artisanal cheeses and bread. To accompany the dinner we bring big dishes of panzanella salad made with heirloom tomatoes, with creamy mozzarella, kalamata olives, capers, and crunchy homemade croutons; orzo salad with fresh, seasonal, roasted vegetables and feta cheese; and always for dessert it must be a homemade wild Maine blueberry pie. The process of packing up, laying out the feast, and sitting as the sun sets over the harbor with chilled wine in our hands (ignoring the mosquitoes that have begun to buzz) can't be beat. We bring all of our "out of town" guests there because we love the tidal creek, and we're sure our guests go home having enjoyed what I believe to be one of the truest quintessential Maine experiences!

Both Jim and I are self-taught cooks and although we own a specialty food company, a café, and a cooking school, and have written seven cookbooks, our real passion is truly for simple comfort meals, updated twists on what we were each raised on in the '60s and '70s as kids in large middle-class families on the outskirts of Boston. We've taken our mothers' recipes and "upgraded" them. We're lucky enough to have access to great ingredients where we live and we believe that's definitely one of the secrets to a memorable meal. Going back to that grilled burger with blue cheese, there are some real steps to making the perfect burger — first of all, we're careful to buy the best meat, just the right ratio of lean to fat and always fresh ground from the local meat market. Always make a little depression in the center of the burger before you put it on the grill; that way it cooks more evenly. We get the coals super hot and prepare the crusty yet soft-in-the-middle bakery buns to grill along with the burgers. We top them with creamy Gorgonzola (Mom wouldn't have done this) or big slices of the best Vermont cheddar, homemade dill pickles, and our favorite chunky ketchup. Hopefully, it's corn season and we can shuck some of the tender, tiny-kernel, sugar and butter ears that are a local favorite. Instead of simply boiling the corn, we take it up a notch and, after parboiling it, we grill it for a couple of minutes on the open fire and then roll each ear in olive oil and balsamic vinegar, sprinkle on freshly grated Parmesan cheese, salt and pepper, and a little crushed mint. Unbelievable! If you really need dessert after this meal, watermelon or a big dish of ice cream hits the spot.

Getting back to my FAVORITE meal ever, before I pick just one I first have to set the scene. It's winter in Maine, a lazy Sunday, and it's been snowing since the night before. The roads aren't too bad yet, but more accumulation is predicted, so we decide to make plans for dinner early in the day to avoid being trapped by the snow. One of us goes to the market, and one of us calls neighbors and friends to see who's brave enough to venture out to Cape Neddick for an early dinner. I'm in my sweats, slippers on my feet, our three goldens, Violet, Daisy, and Lily, are happily hanging around me waiting for me to drop scraps on the floor, and the fire is blazing.

The menu is complete with my favorites: slowly braised short ribs that have been simmering for hours and melt in your mouth, a sumptuous potato gratin, Brussels sprouts roasted in Maine maple syrup, and individual molten chocolate lava cakes are served to finish the night. For me, the key to having a good time is really having the time to spend the entire day in the kitchen pulling out pots and pans, slicing and dicing, and enjoying the aromas as they begin to fill the kitchen. The music is usually playing some oldies. Around 4:00 p.m., I lay out basic white plates, some sparkling glasses, and open a few bottles of wine as I put the finishing touches on my meal.

There's something about slow cooking that I love. Maybe the old saying, "Good things come to those who wait," is true in cooking too. While a quick meal of soup and salad can be terrific, there is something earthy and satisfying about a meal that takes hours to prepare and only gets better the longer it cooks. I think the more we are all rushed in our everyday lives, the more relaxing it is on those rare occasions when we have lots of time to savor the experience. That's why the weather seems to be an important part of this adventure. So if Mother Nature cooperates, late next spring there will be a nor'easter, a heavy snowstorm in the winter, thunderstorms on many hot summer days, and a bitter cold, windy, and damp weekend in November so I can have a good reason, at least a few times next year, to make my most memorable meals again and again and again.

Short Ribs, Bourguignon Style   *Serves 6*

3 strips bacon, cut into pieces

6 meaty short ribs, about 4½ pounds, seasoned with
    salt and pepper just before cooking.

4 carrots, finely chopped

1 medium onion, finely chopped

2 cloves garlic, finely chopped

2 cups dry red wine

3 cups beef or veal stock

2 tablespoons tomato paste

1 (12-ounce) can plum tomatoes, pureed

Sprig or two each of fresh rosemary and thyme

2 bay leaves

1 tablespoon red wine vinegar

1 tablespoon olive oil

1 tablespoon butter

½ pound button mushrooms, quartered

½ pound frozen pearl onions

In a large Dutch oven or 3-to-4-quart pan, sauté bacon pieces to render fat, then remove and reserve bacon for garnish.

In the bacon fat, brown the short ribs on all sides, a few at a time, for 8 to 10 minutes. Set aside lightly covered with aluminum foil.

Add the carrots, onion, and garlic to the pan and sauté until softened, 5 to 7 minutes.

Add the wine and cook for a minute or two. Add the stock, tomato paste, puree, and bring to a boil, and cook down for 5 minutes or so, making sure to scrape up any browned bit on the bottom of the pan.

Add the herbs and vinegar, stir, then return the beef and any accumulated juices to the pan.

Preheat the oven to 250°F. Cover the pan and put into oven for 4 to 5 hours, turning the ribs once or twice during the cooking time.

While the ribs are cooking, you can pre-cook your mushrooms and pearl onions; sauté together in a mixture of 1 tablespoon olive oil and 1 tablespoon butter until browned. Combine and set aside.

When the beef is done, carefully remove from the pan and set aside, covered. Remove the fat with a large spoon from the top of the liquid, then strain the liquid through a fine sieve, gently pushing the vegetables through with the back of the spoon. Put the gravy back on the stove to a simmer and reduce until thickened.

Add the sautéed mushrooms and onions to the thickened gravy. When ready to serve, ladle a generous serving of gravy over the top of the beef and sprinkle with a few pieces of the bacon. Serve with lots of crusty bread

POTATO GRATIN   *Serves 6*

1-pound chunk Parmesan cheese

1 tablespoon olive oil

4 pounds potatoes, peeled and thinly sliced

Salt and freshly ground black pepper

4 tablespoons unsalted butter, cut into small cubes

3 tablespoons all-purpose flour

1 tablespoon fresh rosemary leaves, minced

1 tablespoon fresh thyme leaves, minced

¾ cup whole milk

¾ cup heavy cream

Shave the Parmesan into thin peels with a wide vegetable peeler. Set aside about 2 cups total.

Preheat the oven to 400°F and place the rack in the middle position.

Grease the bottom of a 9 x 14-inch baking dish with the olive oil. Arrange about half of the potatoes in a thin layer on the bottom of the pan. Sprinkle with salt and pepper to taste, half the butter, half the herbs, and half of the Parmesan.

Layer the remaining potatoes and the rest of the butter and herbs. Layer the remaining cheese on top, and pour the milk and cream over the whole dish. Sprinkle with salt and pepper. Bake for 45 minutes. (If the potatoes are getting overly browned, cover them loosely with aluminum foil.)

Reduce the oven temperature to 300° and bake for an additional 30 to 45 minutes, until the potatoes are tender and the cheese is bubbling.

MAPLE-GLAZED BRUSSELS SPROUTS   *Serves 4*

20 to 25 fresh Brussels sprouts

2 tablespoons butter

⅓ cup maple syrup

1 tablespoon curry powder

Clip the ends of the Brussels sprouts and remove outer leaves. Using a food processor fitted with a slicing blade, shred the sprouts. Melt the butter in a sauté pan over medium heat. As soon as the bubbling subsides, add the shredded sprouts. Toss often, being careful not to burn; however, you do want the edges brown. The sprouts will wilt, and the bottom of the pan will have a nice glaze.

When the sprouts are to your liking, drizzle with the maple syrup and dust with the curry powder.

Shauna James Ahern writes the popular Web site Gluten-Free Girl and the Chef (glutenfreegirl.com), which was named one of the best food sites in the world by Gourmet.com, Bon Appetit.com, and the *London Times,* as well as being named one of the "20 Best Blogs By and For Women" by the *Sunday Telegraph.* Gluten-Free Girl and the Chef won Best Food Blog with a Theme in the World in 2006 and receives thousands of hits a day. Shauna's book, *Gluten-Free Girl: How I Found the Food That Loves Me Back and How You Can Too* is now in paperback. Her new book is *Gluten-Free Girl and the Chef: A Love Story in 100 Tempting Recipes,* written with her husband, Daniel.

BUMPING HIPS IN THE KITCHEN

Shauna James Ahern

The first time Danny stepped foot in my kitchen, we cooked together.

We stood in front of the stove and talked, both of us chopping vegetables. My knife skills were pretty well nonexistent — I hacked up onions with a blunt force and intensity that left onion juice squirting over our hands. He didn't say anything. I noted that kindness right away. The rhythm of his knife matched the rhythm of our conversation. He created fine dices of onion, all the same size, while he looked at me and smiled. Seeing him chop enticed me to slow down and watch his technique. As he minced the garlic, I leaned down and took in a whiff: spice and familiar warmth, head rush and clarity.

I'm pretty sure I fell in love with him over the garlic.

Actually, I had fallen in love with him the first time we met, but I had not been willing to admit it yet.

We connected through an online dating site, which made me wince. After three separate spates of dating guys I met on the computer, I was convinced this would never work. Men who were twenty years older than their photo suggested, men who were married and claimed they were single, men who wanted to marry me before we actually met — I had experienced a painful range of people who were not right for me. At thirty-nine, I was ready to give up. In fact, I had emailed all my friends an invitation to my fortieth birthday party with the subject "To Hell with the Wedding Party." I was nearly done.

But after I had the word "yes" tattooed on my wrist, I realized I was open to everything in my life but the possibility that the right man for me could be standing in my kitchen soon. I signed up for an online dating site, once again. (Being a high school English teacher, surrounded by married colleagues and evenings full of grading, I had no luck meeting anyone in the aisle of the grocery store, as all those dating books suggested I would.) I decided to give it six weeks.

Six weeks later, after one date after another that turned into a dud — not one of them loved food — I gave up. *That's it,* I said. *Clearly I'm going to become the woman with all the cats.*

My literary agent had just signed me after reading my food blog. My life was going in that direction. That was my yes.

Curiosity got the better of me. I checked the dating email account one more time, the day before my subscription ran out. Danny's kind eyes were the last ones I saw on the list of men who had written to me. And he was a chef. I said yes one more time.

After a week of brief emails describing our meals and what he was cooking at his restaurant, we met for coffee. Talking with him was like the warm smell of chocolate chip cookies in the kitchen, the familiar feeling of my hand holding a hot cup of coffee, the taste of bacon alongside eggs. I wanted to share every meal with him.

Two weeks later, we stood in the kitchen together. I roasted a chicken stuffed with a hot lemon, a trick I had learned from Jamie Oliver. The skin emerged from the oven crisp and golden brown, the flesh juicy. Danny had roasted yellow peppers and folded them into the creamiest mashed potatoes I had ever eaten. He took a bite of my chicken and ran around the room. (It's awfully fun to impress a chef with your food.) I ate his yellow pepper mashed potatoes and yelled out a little hallelujah. We kissed. We fed each other more food. We danced together.

The fact that it all had to be gluten-free for me didn't faze him at all.

A few weeks after that first meal, I asked him to move in with me. (He made a tremendous frisée salad with warm bacon vinaigrette and a poached egg, minus the traditional croutons.) A few weeks after that, he asked me to marry him. (That happened over pan-seared beef tenderloin with potato purée and balsamic onions.) The next summer, he stood in the kitchen of the next house we shared, frosting the chocolate-banana cake I had made the night before with a rich chocolate ganache. Two hours later, we were married. And when we brought our daughter home from the hospital, we stood at the stove as she slept and made berry jam with all the summer fruit that friends had dropped off on our doorstep as her welcome.

We haven't stopped cooking since that first meal we created together. We never will.

About the Editor

MARK CHIMSKY-LUSTIG is editor-in-chief of the book division of Sellers Publishing. For eight years, he ran his own editorial consulting business. Previously he was executive editor and editorial director of Harper San Francisco and headed the paperback divisions at Little, Brown and Macmillan. In addition, he was on the faculty of New York University's Center for Publishing and for three years he served as the director of the book section of NYU's Summer Publishing Institute. He has edited a number of bestselling books and worked with such authors as Johnny Cash, Melody Beattie, Susie Bright, Robert Funk, Arthur Hertzberg, Beryl Bender Birch, and Robert Coles. He is an award-winning poet whose poetry and essays have appeared in *JAMA* (*The Journal of the American Medical Association*), *Three Rivers Poetry Journal,* and *Mississippi Review.* He has developed and compiled *Creating a Marriage You'll Love* and *Creating a Life You'll Love,* which was a *Maine Sunday Telegram* bestseller and winner of the silver in *ForeWord's* 2009 Book of the Year Awards (self-help category).

ACKNOWLEDGMENTS

Creating a Meal You'll Love is the newest book in a series that began with *Creating a Life You'll Love* and was followed by *Creating a Marriage You'll Love*, all published by Sellers Publishing. The idea for this book came from Charlotte Smith at Sellers, who has worked her production magic on each of the books in this series. I want to thank the entire Sellers team for offering ideas for chefs and food writers and for sharing their insights, ideas, and enthusiastic support for this project. In particular, I owe a special debt of gratitude to Ronnie Sellers, President and Publisher, Robin Haywood, Publishing Director, and Mary Baldwin, Managing Editor, as well as Megan Hiller, Senior Editor (and resident cookbook expert), who made numerous beneficial recommendations and patiently answered every culinary question, large and small, from this rookie in the world of food writing. It's been said before but it bears repeating: It takes a village.

The process of assembling an anthology that contains many original pieces makes one adept at coaxing, cajoling, and persevering. Once commitments are made, there is always that next phase of trying to get all the essays in before the book is due to go to the printer. In this regard I want to thank all the contributors who said yes and then followed through by delivering wonderful essays to this collection — its sales will benefit the efforts of Share Our Strength® to end childhood hunger in America. I am also grateful to Nava Atlas, Susan RoAne, Patti Breitman, Charlotte Senn, Sarah Abell, Lucinda East, Elizabeth Kellogg, Ann Miller, Joy Pierson, Brianna Cook, Joy Tutela, Jane Dystel, Miriam Goderich, Kris Dahl, Laura Neely, and Ron Longe for their generous assistance.

Also, my deep appreciation to Rita Sowins, to Stacey Cramp, to Faceout Studio, and to Pam Hoenig, for her invaluable proofreading.

Last, but not least, I want to thank Kimberly Gladman for her wise literary counsel and friendship, Haya Leah Molnar, Joanna Laufer, Laurie Moore Skillings, Richard Morse, Dede Byster, Christine Dietz, Linda McKenney, and my son, who gave me a food memory to cherish when one night he offered to make me dinner and created a meal that I loved.

ALSO AVAILABLE FROM SELLERS PUBLISHING:

Creating a Life You'll Love
An inspiring, thought-provoking collection of some
of the best commencement addresses of recent years
by such notables as Genevieve Bell, Wendell Berry,
Ken Burns, Thomas L. Friedman, Tess Gerritsen, Dana
Gioia, Tom Hanks, Molly Ivins, Barbara Kingsolver, Ray
Kurzweil, David Levering Lewis, David McCullough,
Harold Prince, Anna Quindlen, Anna Deavere Smith,
Karen Tse, and Muhammad Yunus. A perfect gift for new
graduates or anyone making a major life transition.

All royalties generated from the sale of this book will
be donated to nonprofit organizations dedicated to
HIV/AIDS prevention and research.

Creating a Marriage You'll Love
Renowned authors and relationship experts provide
insights and valuable advice on how to achieve long-
lasting happiness and fulfillment in marriage, with essays
by such distinguished contributors as Nava Atlas, Joseph
Bailey, Kristine Carlson, Nicole Chaison, Barbara
De Angelis, Debra Galant, John Gray, Gay Hendricks,
Harriet Lerner, Mike Robbins, and Judith Wallerstein.

All royalties generated from the sale of this book will be
donated to nonprofit organizations dedicated to helping
victims of domestic violence.

CREDITS

"The Tastes of Christmas Past" © 2010 J. Horak-Druiff; "Food Memories" © 2010 Denise Vivaldo; "Dinner at Richard's" © 2010 Nick Malgieri; "Inspired by an Ideal Meal: A Love Story of Family, Food, and Good Fortune" © 2010 Susur Lee; "Cooking by Cable" © 2010 David Sax; "The Most Important Meal of the Day" © 2010 Amy Sherman; "A Sweet End" © 2010 Jansen Chan; "Dinner with the Barone and the Baronessa" © 2010 Mary Ann Esposito, recipe for Timballo di Melanzine e Bucatini from *Ciao Italia Slow and Easy* by Mary Ann Esposito, © 2007 by the author and reprinted by permission of St. Martin's Press, LLC; "For Old Time's Sake" © 2010 Mimi Sheraton; "A High-Stakes Game of Hot Pot"© 2010 Steamy Kitchen Inc.; "It All Ends in Samba" © 2010 Leticia Moreinos Schwartz, recipe from *The Brazilian Kitchen* by Leticia Moreinos Schwartz, © 2010. Used by permission from Kyle Books.; "All's Well That Eats Well" © 2010 Bart Potenza, recipe reprinted from *The Candle Cafe Cookbook* by Joy Pierson and Bart Potenza with Barbara Scott-Goodman (Clarkson Potter), © 2003 by Joy Pierson and Bart Potenza. Used by permission of Clarkson Potter/Publishers, an imprint of the Crown Publishing Group, a division of Random House, Inc.; "Feeding the Soul and the Senses" © 2010 Mika Takeuchi; "Lasagna You'll Love" © 2010 Ronald Holden; "Crêpe Complète" © 2010 Louisa Chu; "Who Is at the Table?" © 2010 Anna Thomas. All Rights Reserved; "Memories of Meals Gone By" © Skye Gyngell; "A Favorite Magic Meal" © 2010 Tracey Ryder; "Lessons from Papa" © 2010 Wendy Lyn; "The Last Supper" © 2010 Karen J. Coates; "Brahmin Soul Food: A Father's One-Way Journey to the Life Hereafter" © 2010 Raghavan Iyer; "White-Apron Syndrome" © 2010 Michael Paley; "An Ode to Julia" © 2010 Julee Rosso Associates, Inc./Wickwood Inn; "My Favorite Spaghetti Recipe" introduction and recipe reprinted from *New American Table* © 2009 by Marcus Samuelsson. Used by permission of John Wiley & Sons Inc.; "My Life, My Meal" © 2010 Michael Laiskonis; "A Summer's Hidden Gem and a Winter's Feast" © 2010 Jonathan King; "Bumping Hips in the Kitchen" © 2010 Shauna James Ahern.